RAVISHED

D1111232

notes on womanhood | heather king

Published by Holy Hell Books

www.heather-king.com

Cover and interior design by DoubleMRanch Design

www.doublemranch.com

Published in the United States of America

ISBN: 978-0578439617

To my sisters:

near and far; past, present, and future

"Take me to you, imprison me, for I,
Except you enthrall me, never shall be free,
Nor ever chaste, except you ravish me."

—John Donne, Holy Sonnet 14

"Women of the entire universe, whether Christian or non-believing,
you to whom life is entrusted at this grave moment in history,
it is for you to save the peace of the world."

—Pope Paul VI, at the conclusion of the Second Vatican Council

"Since the day of my conversion, I have never been well."

—St. Francis of Assisi

TABLE OF CONTENTS

IV. RADICAL FREEDOM, RADICAL EXILE

ENDNOTES

RAVISHED

PREFACE

I'm an ex-gutter drunk who graduated from law school in a blackout, sobered up, quit my job as a Beverly Hills litigation attorney, converted to Catholicism, and in the mid-1990's embarked on the precarious life of a creative writer. My history includes promiscuity, abortions, adultery, a 14-year marriage that ended in divorce, and a life-long tendency toward romantic obsession.

Divorced, childless, single, aging, as a woman, in and out of the Church, I often feel I have nowhere to lay my head.

In and out of the Church as well, I'm also often challenged by my fellow women to be angrier. "How can you belong to a church that won't allow female priests?" for example, is a question I hear often. The short answer is because Christ set it up that way. The long answer is that just because men do something women should be able to do it, and vice versa, is a notion that strikes me as moronic. I want to glorify womanhood, not water it down. Any woman who wants to be a priest for the right reasons—which is to die to self, to serve—will already have naturally ordered her life so as to be acting in a priestly capacity.

Beneath the anger is fear. Beneath the anger is the one fact we're really not "allowed" to say: that we long with all our hearts for the male gaze. To live with the tension of not having that gaze returned with the intensity we ache for, or maybe at all—and to react with patience, kindness, and creative nonviolence, while still loving men—that is the way of the real warrior and the real feminist.

So is trying to be kind, understanding, and compassionate to all women: the pregnant teenager, the trans recovering alcoholic, the gun-toting, home-schooling Republican.

To hold such tension, all our lives, is the way of suffering. Not dumb, wearily-resigned suffering, but active, conscious suffering. "Stay awake!" said Christ. And before we start pointing the finger at everyone else, let's remember that, being human, every one of us comes to the table with our egos, our agendas, our wounds. Even those of us sufficiently well-educated, well-traveled, and well-experienced perhaps to consider ourselves above the fray come with deep vulnerabilities and fears: that we're not pretty enough, thin enough, loud enough, quiet enough. To acknowledge our vulnerabilities and fears—and to devote our lives to trying to live fully with many of them intact—is the way of strength, not weakness.

Many of us come with a hard-wired propensity to "pick" and then to compulsively pursue emotionally unavailable men.

For most of my life, I've counted myself squarely among that last group. In fact, to have longed for a man and never to have had a truly reciprocal, healthy loving relationship with a man—partly because I've been blueprinted for another vocation, partly because my own temperament has engineered against it—is my deepest, tenderest wound.

My "failure" at romance is the part of my story that tends to make me feel most ashamed, humiliated, exiled, and like a loser. It touches upon my fear that I'm not worthy of love nor capable of loving others. It goes to the heart of my womanhood and my humanity.

To accept this reality—to have come to see my situation, even, as a strange grace—has been a long, painful crucifixion. But to have suffered the wound these last three decades without anesthesia—no matter how lonely, frustrated, and crazy I've felt; never knowing how long the suffering might last—has formed in me, at last, something useful, something eternal.

I want to tell the story of those years of purification.

I want to tell of what has been the adventure, the pilgrimage, the gamble of my life.

Here's what I've learned: Our deepest identity does not lie in our gender, our sexual orientation, our wounds.

Our identity lies in Christ.

ALL THIS JUICE AND ALL THIS JOY

"What is all this juice and all this joy?
A strain of the earth's sweet being in the beginning
In Eden garden. – Have, get, before it cloy,
Before it cloud, Christ, lord, and sour with sinning,
Innocent mind and Mayday in girl and boy,
Most, O maid's child, thy choice and worthy the winning."

—GERARD MANLEY HOPKINS, FROM "SPRING"

FIDELITY AND FREEDOM

I'm 66, single, childless.

I've never been financially supported by a man.

I've made my way in two traditionally male worlds: the law and publishing.

I've been the recipient of women's rights—for the vote, for equal pay—and I'm deeply grateful. I'm appalled by the continuing discrimination against and violence toward women, the world over.

But I don't think the solution to our anguish—as women, as human beings—is to clamor that we're the same as men and to go around being resentful at them. I think the solution, and I speak as an educated, Western woman of privilege, is to acknowledge the ways we women contribute to, cooperate with, and foster the objectification of women, and then to change our own behavior.

If I want to lower the incidence of rape, for example, I get to stop using the other, and letting myself be used, as an object. If I want men to stop oppressing my sisters, I get to look at the way I oppress others: emotionally, socially, financially, spiritually.

I think we need to ponder the roots of violence and to soften and purify our own hearts. I think we need to be kinder to men and kinder and way gentler with each other.

I think we way need a better sense of humor.

Most of all, I think we need to accurately name things. I'm a child of the '60s and '70s. Women's liberation was not liberating, not for our hearts, not for our souls. Free love exacts a very high price.

We give ourselves away—physically, emotionally, spiritually—then blame men for making us feel cheap.

We cede our wombs to pharmaceutical companies, and then decry genital mutilation across the world.

We cede our nervous systems and brains to the manufacturers of psychotropic drugs, and then blame men for being stupid and insensitive.

We binge-watch TV shows in which men and women ceaselessly demean each other, then cry foul when men demean us in real life. We watch, promote, and condone films with extreme sex and extreme violence, and are then outraged when the male creators of such "entertainment" exhibit "sexual misconduct" toward the women who are jockeying to be hired as the entertainers. We hang out on social media all day making snarky comments, then blame men for being warmongers.

We shame men for helping us, and then blame them for not helping us enough, or in the right way.

The effect has been to drive a wedge between the sexes, and between each other, that has caused more suffering, loneliness and oppression for women than perhaps at any other time in history.

A certain strain of Catholic culture sometime seems to believe that we need to add a bit of an edge to the teachings of the Gospels. A certain strain of thought holds that Christ isn't quite fierce enough, aware enough, contemporary enough, radical enough.

Are you kidding me? Christ—God made man who consented to take on human form, pitched his tent among us, spoke truth to every power and principality of his (and our) day, ate, drank, told stories, healed, wandered, loved; a totally "ordinary" man, unrecognized as the Messiah by his own people, who addressed and touched on every facet of the human person: existential, philosophical, theological, eschatological; who drank to the last bitter drop the fatigue and loneliness and bewilderment and terror and sorrow of the human condition; who was crucified, died, was buried and rose again on the third day leaving us his Body and Blood to eat?

Christ trumped for all time all edginess, all weirdness, all fierceness, all desire or attempt to be "radical." Anything other or less than Christ waters down, makes insipid, diminishes the Way, the Truth and the Life: the one Way, the only Truth, the highest possible Life.

My fidelity to the teachings of the Gospels, however awkward and stumbling, means I don't need to be told I'm "strong" or to trumpet the fact that I'm strong: I know I'm strong. And my strength, such as it is, lies precisely in my poverty of spirit, my utter dependence on God, the acceptance of my complete inability to heal my own wounds, to eradicate my own limitations, or to fulfill the deepest desires of my own heart.

🍐 THE HEMORRAGING WOMAN

They go out, they go out, full of tears,
carrying seed for the sowing:
they come back, they come back, full of song,
carrying their sheaves.

—Psalm 126

I've told my conversion story in *Redeemed: Stumbling Towards God, Marginal Sanity, and the Peace That Passes All Understanding.*

Briefly, back in the early '90s, newly sober, newly married, new to LA, I worked for a time as a Beverly Hills lawyer.

I had a crisis of conscience and of vocation. My concerns were not, however, political; they were religious. As Simone Weil said, "One cannot imagine St. Francis of Assisi speaking of rights." Instead my questions were: What is my purpose on earth? Who and what do I want to serve?

Desperate for answers, for meaning, and with zero "theological" background, I began to read the Gospels on my lunch hour at work. The Gospels were the living water that led me to Christ. Christ said, "Do not think that I have come to abolish the law or the prophets. I have come not to abolish but to fulfill" [Matthew 5:17]. He said to bring into the storehouse both the old and the new.

I saw that Christ called men and women in very different ways. To the men, he said, "Follow me." But the women got him right away. Jesus got women and women got him. He got what we will do out of our longing for relationship. He got what we will do to men, to each other, and to ourselves.

He got the way our yearning for love can turn into the wrong kind of "crazy love:" obsession, codependence, putting up with abusive behavior. I myself had been walking the thin line between passion and pathology all my life.

I was struck by the many Gospel parables in which Jesus encounters, heals, protects, and ministers to women.

The woman caught in adultery [John 8:1-11].

The woman at the well [John 4:1-42].

The woman who'd been crippled for eighteen years who Christ healed on a Sunday [Luke 13: 10-17].

The woman who said, "Even the dogs eat scraps." [Matthew 15:21-28].

Hid deep friendship with Martha and Mary [Luke 10:38-42].

The widow who gave her last two mites [Luke 21:1-4].

The woman who washed Christ's feet with her tears [Luke 7:36-50].

The women who discovered the empty tomb [Luke 24:1-9]. This is so true to life. We would be hanging about: "checking in," just wanting to "be there." Christ is always available to us. Christ is always dying for us to sit with him for an hour. And we women are often the first to notice the Resurrection.

Mary Magdalene, who met Christ in the garden after his Resurrection. "Mary," he said. "Rabboni," she replied—surely one of the most touching and intimate exchanges ever recorded between a woman and a man.

His mother Mary of course—who he crowned Queen of Heaven and Earth.

How could anyone say the Church didn't love women!

But the parable to which I most deeply responded was that of the hemorrhaging woman who touched the hem of Christ's garment and was healed [Luke 8:40-56; Mark 5: 25-35]. A woman, much less a woman who was hemorrhaging, i.e. "unclean," would have been forbidden to touch a rabbi in any way. In fact, she could have stood to be stoned to death for doing so.

"But the woman fearing and trembling, knowing what was done in her, came and fell down before him, and told him all the truth. And he said unto her, 'Daughter, thy faith hath made thee whole; go in peace, and be whole of thy plague.'" [Mark 5:33-34].

I'd had many plagues in my life.

And at the corner of Wilshire and Doheny, gazing longingly out the window of my 6th floor law office, I saw that Christ, the Great Physician, had been nursing me—tenderly, surely—all along.

THY FAITH HATH MADE THEE WHOLE

Christ never tried to extinguish the glorious distinction between men and women. He acknowledges the distinction, calls us higher; treats us women as partners, equals, companions.

How easy Christ was with women! How integrated. How comfortable. He didn't flinch, even when the misfit, over-emoting streetwalker dried his feet with her hair. In fact, he loved people who were willing to step outside the lines and make fools of themselves. He of all people knew our fear of being made fun of, of being called losers and weirdos.

He of all people knew the poverty of womanhood.

He didn't patronize or condescend.

He invited us, too, to drink from the chalice.

When I got married in 1990, I didn't know I'd convert six years later, and that eight years after that, the marriage would end—at my behest—in divorce and annulment. I didn't know that remaining faithful to the teachings of the Church after the divorce would mean 18 years and counting of celibacy. Eighteen years ago, I would not, given the choice, have freely chosen celibacy. What I did freely choose was fidelity to the Church, my Mother.

That fidelity has led to a life of prayer, the vocation of writing, and a kind of cockeyed off-the-grid "ministry" in which I am a mother, sister, daughter, and friend to many.

My fidelity has led to an interior freedom such that feeling discriminated against, belittled, or minimized by men is simply not on my radar. There are certain men who make me feel that way or, more accurately, who I allow to let me feel that way. Sometimes that's because I've assigned the guy the impossible task of making me feel happy or secure. In that case, my responsibility has been to do the years of inner work and prayer that have enabled me to find my happiness, such as it is, and security in God.

Certain men in publishing have at times tried to bully me or railroad me or pay me less than I'm worth. In that case, my responsibility, again, has been to learn how to negotiate, make boundaries, and ask for what I'm worth without fear of appearing pushy or aggressive. If a publisher or parish or magazine can't afford me, or to meet my terms, I'm able to say so pleasantly and to move on.

The culture is rigid, not the Church. Christ sets us free. Around men, here's what that freedom, in my experience, looks like. I don't have to be a milquetoast, weirdly submissive, codependent, cringing, toadying, seductive, or false. I also don't have to be aggressive, abrasive, chip-on-my-shoulder, out to prove myself, vengeful, or evidence-gathering. I can be more or less myself and I won't be looking to men to tell me who that might be.

I can stand my ground when necessary and I also delight in men, admire men, see where men are wounded, support men. Of course certain of them will be irksome. Of course each interaction and friendship is an ongoing challenge and adventure.

Of course my heart continues to be pierced by the wound between women and men.

But I'm not sentenced to waste my time complaining, or feeling sorry for myself, or trying to browbeat men or any particular man into changing.

I get to change. Plus I'm busy going about my own tragicomic, infinitely absorbing life.

❧ THE SILENCE OF CHRIST

Again, I am so not a woman who is angry at the Church.

I'd spent so many years wandering around absolutely broken, and fallen, and squandering my inheritance in the mire, that my sense of the Church from the beginning was, I can't believe there's a place for me still laid at the table. I can't believe I've been welcomed home…I can't believe I even managed to find my way home…

Afterward, I realized that the family I'd been welcomed into was just as broken in some ways as I was, and that the brokenness was to be noticed, and acknowledged, and mourned, and addressed. That didn't make me any less inclined to love the Church and to follow Christ, though. If anything, in fact, the Church's brokenness made me identify with it more, including its slowness to admit its problems and take full responsibility for them, but also including its efforts to keep "showing up" in spite of its glaring and varied faults.

Imperfect though the Church can be, Catholicism doesn't insult the intelligence by asking anyone to believe reality to be other than exactly as it is. Christ on the Cross acknowledges right up front that life consists largely of failure, rejection, pain, loss; that we are often not treated with the charity we feel we deserve; the family often isn't reconciled, the cancer often doesn't go into remission.

Christianity doesn't ask: Why isn't life "fair?" It asks: What kind of shape are you going to be in to comfort the next person who's in pain? How are you going to make your way through a world that worships money? How are you going to face aging and death?—because even if everyone treats you exactly the way you want them to, which they never do, you're still going to die.

With all that, in the face of the brokenness of the Church and the unspeakable violence of our culture, when to speak and when to keep silent requires an agonizing process of ongoing discernment. Christ himself said so little! I think that's because when you're truly willing and ready to lay down your life, you don't talk about it. You just do it, live it.

Christ simply was, is.

He embodied truth.

He was love incarnate.

To that end, his whole public ministry was a form of "speaking out." He healed on Sundays. He stood with the criminal (for example, the adulterous woman). He upset the status quo of money, property and prestige —especially spiritual prestige (e.g., when he drove the money-changers from the temple). He put himself in a place of constant vulnerability, constant risk, and mortal peril.

I wonder if when, as he so often did, he went off to a lonely place to pray, he was not praying to guard his own heart from violence. How hard it must have been not to give in to the temptation to slap the faces of the hypocrites, the nitpicking rule-followers whose hearts were so out for themselves that they could not, did not, refused to see the goodness and holiness of Christ. How hard it must have been to refrain from retaliating against the Pharisees who followed him about spying, like the hateful blackguards they were, trying to catch out love incarnate, perpetually weaving their nets of lies.

He wasn't afraid to call them hypocrites and liars, again at mortal peril to himself. But in the end, his main emotion was sorrow: "O Jerusalem, Jerusalem...how often would I have gathered thy children together, even as a hen gathereth her chickens under her wings, and ye would not!" [Matthew 23:37].

One of the things Christ must have learned in the thirty years before his public ministry is that no amount of discussion or reasoning will convert the human heart that is closed. If you hunger and thirst for goodness, beauty, truth, you will fall upon the Gospels weeping with joy. If you don't, you will resolutely, steadfastly deny them, or worse, try to twist them to support your own ends, insisting that "Love thine enemies" actually means to arm yourself with assault weapons against them, and that "Blessed are the poor in spirit" actually means "Blessed are the prosperous."

So again we return to the scandal of the Cross: of praying in secret, of hungering and thirsting for justice, of quietly and mostly invisibly consenting to the ongoing Crucifixion of trying to live out our smallest moments in love. Failing most of the time, of course, but still.

As always, Christ is the answer. "I am the vine, you are the branches. Whoever remains in me and I in him will bear much fruit, because without me you can do nothing" [John 15:5].

Nothing!

THE EIGHTH STATION OF THE CROSS

I grew up on the coast of New Hampshire. Since childhood, I've been captivated by the ocean. Since childhood, I've felt compelled by the infinite horizon.

My first kiss was near the ocean.

I first told a guy "I love you" while walking along the shore of the ocean.

In 1990, newly sober, newly married, I moved to another ocean, another shore. In 1996, I converted to Catholicism and came into the Church. In 1999, my father died. In 2000, I was diagnosed with breast cancer. In 2001, I was divorced and had my marriage annulled. In 2010, I sought healing for the abortions I'd had over twenty years before. In 2012, my mother died.

For years, I'd set aside an hour or two each morning for prayer. I read, pondered, and wrote about the Way, the Truth and the Life of Christ. I devoted many hours a week to staying sober and helping another alcoholic to achieve sobriety.

And in July, 2014, I decided to go back to the coast of Massachusetts, general site of my deepest childhood, sexual, and emotional wounds. I signed up to do a 30-day retreat, based on the spiritual exercises of St. Ignatius of Loyola.

A few days in, I was walking a footpath in the woods when I came upon the Stations of the Cross.

I'd prayed the Stations many times over the years, usually during Lent, without paying especially close attention. But recently I'd felt moved to buy a little laminated card, imprinted with the appropriate numbers and prayers, which I happened to be carrying in my back pocket. I'd thought, dimly, to commit all fourteen to memory.

This particular set of Stations consisted of simple, open-faced wooden boxes with small metal bas-reliefs: Station One: Jesus Is Condemned to Death. Station Two: Jesus Takes Up His Cross.

Each was nailed to a tree and the trees formed a double row: a kind of grassy allée that ran down to the ocean. The woods were alive with the sound of birdsong, the skittering of small mammals, the low hum of insects.

So I had my little card, and I was going along, praying. And at Station Eight—"Jesus Speaks to the Women"—I was unexpectedly overcome. Between the second and third time that he fell, Jesus spoke to the women.

I'd never reflected that, according to tradition, the women were the last people Christ met before he fell to the ground beneath his burden, was stripped of his garments and was nailed to the cross. We all like to look good in front of the opposite sex, but at that point he would have been at his absolute worst: his weakest, his most vulnerable, his most physically grotesque. And yet he stopped. He spoke to the women.

Who better understood weakness, vulnerability, the fear of looking unattractive, the desire to love and be loved, than Jesus? Who, in other words, better understood women than Christ?

Jesus spoke to the women. He was speaking still. He'd been speaking to me, personally, all along.

The intensity of my reaction shocked me. I felt a stab of melting intimacy, a rock-bottom sense that as an aging, childless, spouseless woman, I was wanted and needed and loved, by him at least, if not by the world.

It may have been the first time I definitively realized that my long, long, pilgrimage toward purity of heart, purity of motives, the slow burning away of all in me that was self-absorbed, self-obsessed, and selfish was not just about me; not even primarily about me.

It was the moment I realized that for over two decades, I'd been writing about and trying to work out what it means to be a woman walking with Christ.

It was the moment I thought: I should collect those thoughts into a book.

A week later, I noticed a huge bull's-eye rash on my stomach, went to the ER, and was diagnosed with Lyme disease.

Very funny, Jesus. I'm pretty sure that deer tick bit me while I was kneeling in the woods, weeping.

🍐 OUR VOCATION IS LOVE

Later that week I learned one version of what Christ actually said when he spoke to the women: "Jesus turned to them and said, "Daughters of Jerusalem, do not weep for me; weep instead for yourselves and for your children, for indeed, the days are coming when people will say, 'Blessed are the barren, the wombs that never bore and the breasts that never nursed'" [Luke 23:28-29].

Don't weep for me, in other words. Weep for yourself and for your sons and daughters. He wasn't pissed or bitter, though. He really meant it. And when we contemplate our hearts hemorrhaging for love, our over- and way-too-early sexualized children, and the global movement toward co-opting the dignity and nobility of women—from human trafficking to the cosmetic surgery industry to the scientific effort to create human life outside and without the need of the female human body—we see exactly what he meant.

Even later in the retreat, I came across Luke 8:3 in my King James Bible. The women who followed Jesus "ministered unto him of their substance."

The women ministered to him of their substance. Not just money —though that, too—but their substance.

I'm not sure there is any higher, kinder or better thing we can do than simply to sit with one another in our suffering. To be truly present. To listen. To receive. That is what giving from our substance consists in. That's what Christ did with his disciples at the Last Supper. That's what the women were doing for Christ on his way to Calvary. That's what Mary did at the foot of the Cross.

That's part of what we women are called to do with and for each other.

The Resurrection doesn't make us "mindful," calm, perfect, effective, suave.

It makes us, in our brokenness, available to and present for other suffering human beings.

To believe that what is so small, so hidden, so seemingly ineffective is actually salvific requires, in my experience, years of prayer, nearly superhuman patience, and the holding of an almost unbearable amount of tension.

As St. Thérèse of Lisieux observed: "I have found my vocation at last: in the heart of my mother the Church I will be love...like that I will be everything... and so my dream will be fulfilled."

That's my dream, too.

The Church has never done anything but foster it.

II

POOR BABY: A CHILD OF THE 60s LOOKS BACK ON ABORTION

Etymology

Latin

From aborior ("pass away; miscarry"), from ab ("of, by, from") + orior.

(Classical) IPA: / `o.ri.or /

Verb

Present active orior, present infinitive orīrī, perfect active ortus sum.
(deponent)

1.   *I rise, get up.*

2.   *I appear, become visible.*

3.   *I am born, come to exist, originate.*

I came of age during the '60's and '70's. I'm a former waitress, an ex-lawyer, a sober drunk, and a self-supporting writer. I've been financially independent all my life. But I've never much been able to reduce the mystical to the political. I've never been much moved to call myself a feminist. The feminists had said that sleeping around would be empowering. The feminists had maintained that "choosing" would make me free. The feminists had asserted that there'd be no repercussions. The feminists had been wrong.

The feminists had been wrong, but I'd always known they were wrong. Every guy I'd ever slept with, for example, no matter how inappropriate or unavailable, I'd pretty much instantly wanted to be my boyfriend, if not marry. What was the matter with me? I'd wondered for a long time. Why did I have to be such a sap? Later, I'd realized you *should* have feelings for the person with whom you have sex. Later—too late—I'd realize you should have feelings for the kid, or in my case kids, you'd conceived.

Through getting sober, getting married, moving from Boston to LA, a (mercifully brief) legal career, quitting my job to become a writer, a divorce, my first book, my second book, I had flourished. I had survived. My life had meaning and point. Los Angeles—so maddening, so glorious—was a fount of the paradoxes on which my creative imagination thrived. I rented a beautiful apartment in a bad part of town. I took long, solitary walks through my over-crowded neighborhood and cooked elaborate dinners for friends. I trudged to Mass, and I drove to the women's jail in Watts and talked to the inmates about addiction.

I complained about the cacophony of ice cream trucks, car alarms, leaf blowers, and hordes of screaming children, and I also knew that the riotous mass of humanity against which I rubbed provided the tension necessary to create and maintain my inner life. I wrote—above all, I wrote—and while I waited for a crumb of news from my agent, I availed myself of the public library, the strip-mall pho joints, the thrift stores with their five-buck Levis and leather jackets, the light that streamed down from the mountains like a benediction.

I was absorbed, energized, engaged. I was not depressed. I did not need or want medication. But beneath the surface ran a searing, aching loneliness, a subliminal sense of sorrow so acute that I once looked up the word "keen" in order to confirm that "a prolonged wail for a deceased person" was indeed the sound silently emanating from one corner of my heart.

I had done what I could to ease the pain. I had told of my past, if the part in question only glancingly, to spiritual directors and friends. A Catholic convert, I had of course come clean in Confession. What was done was done—and yet, one part of my face I could never show; one part of my psyche was so shrouded in darkness that even I, who make a life's work of pondering, analyzing, contemplating, could not fully access it.

That I instinctively avoided children, tensed up when passing toy stores and playgrounds, blanched at the phrase "baby shower"

I had come to accept as simply part of my hard-wiring. Finally, however, I made the connection that I couldn't, or wouldn't, make before. I realized that the three abortions I'd had over two decades earlier were not fading increasingly into the background, as I'd kept expecting, but claiming ever more of my attention.

We're very concerned these days that everyone is given a "voice," but one person nobody wants to hear from is the woman who's had an abortion. One side says: *What I do in bed is my business*; the other side says: *You made your bed, now lie in it*. The left doesn't want to hear from the woman who's had an abortion because to feel remorse, shame, or doubt is to betray "the cause." The right doesn't want to hear from the woman who's had an abortion because you're going to burn in hell so why should *you* matter? The priest doesn't want to hear, particularly, from the woman who's had an abortion because the issue is way too complex, multi-layered, and potentially time-consuming; women, as we all know, get weird around sex, men, and children; the priest, being human, may not have worked all those things out within himself (to be fair, who has?), and besides, *you've been forgiven*, so let's forego opening that can of worms and move on.

Even women, who will talk about *anything*, don't talk about abortion. Women, who within five minutes of meeting will know each other's career, relationship status, family situation, taste in clothing, food, movies, books, and men, don't talk about abortion. I think this is because women, of all people, know that abortion is a failure of love. Women know that if the guy with whom you were sleeping loved you enough, chances are you would have had his baby in a heartbeat. Women know that no matter how superficially relieved you may have felt afterwards; no matter how financially, emotionally, and logistically impossible having a kid just then would have been; no matter how much sympathy they may (or may not) have for you and your situation, you've still gone against your deepest soul: everything in you that is most precious, most worthy, most inviolate.

The fact that I had so egregiously gone against my own deepest soul lay squarely, forever, with me. I did not blame the women's movement. I did not blame the men I had slept with. But I did begin to see that, as contemplative writer Ron Rolheiser has observed: "In a culture which is sexually irresponsible the inevitable losers are women. They end up suffering the most."

This is not a political idea; it's a human idea: which is to say an idea leading away from victim-hood and toward maturity. Maturity means consenting to develop a conscience. Maturity means acknowledging that our actions always have consequences; our choices always have repercussions. Maturity compelled me to admit that sexual responsibility had hardly been *my* forte: the fathers of the first two children I'd aborted had both been married. And the father of the third child I aborted I'd been engaged to marry myself.

I once did a radio interview in which the conversation turned to abortion. Afterward, the host said, "Forgive me, but since you went the easy route by not having children, people might think it's hypocritical for you to speak on abortion. You may not quite have the *right* to a voice." That's one way of looking at it. Another would be that women who have had abortions are the *most* qualified to speak. If not me—and women like me—who, then?

The woman who didn't have an abortion and regrets it? Bring her on. Let's see the woman who is dying to point to her kid and tell the world: *This is the biggest mistake of my life. I'd give her away now if I could. The world would be a richer, more joyful, more peaceful place had I destroyed my daughter in the womb.*

Bring that woman on if you can find her. Bring all such women on. You're going to find very, very few, if any, because we all know that *once you have the kid, you will love him or her. And then where will you be?* We all know what happens when you love someone. You turn into a fool! You make crazy sacrifices! You do without all kinds of things that in your right mind you wouldn't dream of doing without! "There is only one thing I dread," said Dostoevsky: "not to be worthy of my sufferings." Maybe I don't have a right to talk about abortion in the sense that I was not at the time worthy of my suffering. But surely we always have a right to say: *I was not worthy of my suffering, and I wish I had been.*

When we talk about abortion we are really talking about the function and meaning of suffering, which is why everybody tends to get so hot under the collar when the subject is raised. The most radical, most incendiary, most taboo subject in our culture is not sex or money or politics or God, but suffering. Nothing will get you killed faster than suggesting that the meaning of life is to be found in our relationship to suffering. Nothing challenges the existing order more; nothing so strongly threatens our bodily, mental, emotional and spiritual integrity; nothing makes us so proprietary about our identity, our organizing principles.

Everyone likes to think, Of course *I'm* compassionate. Of course *my* life is geared toward alleviating suffering. But most of the time our lives are only geared in that direction if we're going to gain by our actions, if we're serving ourselves. When we see the terrible, endless suffering of the world we don't tend to think, for example, *Let me forego this act that would bring me instant gratification but that is not toward the greater good.* We don't tend to think, *Let me take the beam out of my own eye before I try to take the beam out of my neighbor's eye.* We don't tend to ask ourselves, *How honest am I, how vulnerable, how selfish?* We tend to think, I'd like to be less selfish, but the world isn't set up that way. We tend to think, *You go first. You change, and then maybe I'll change. You be vulnerable, and then I'll be vulnerable. You stop waging war, and then I'll stop waging war. But first—let's have sex!*

I began to realize that there had to be legions of women— and possibly men—walking around bearing the same harrowing, isolating burden I was. I began, tentatively, to broach the subject to people I knew. Female friends of decades-long standing confided that they, too, had had an abortion (or more than one); they, too, had kept their feelings and thoughts under wraps. One friend with three grown children was still haunted by the abortion she'd had as a teenager. Another, though wanting the child, had had an abortion at the insistence of her partner, only to be promptly dumped, then watch the guy go off, find a hotter, younger babe, proceed to father a whole family, and by all accounts live happily ever after.

Maybe the most wrenching conversation was with a man, a film critic and former junkie. He said his wife had had multiple abortions before they were married. He said she'd been to a slew of therapists since, but had never made her peace. He said he himself had never quite recovered from the unilateral decision of a long-ago ex-girlfriend to abort the child they'd conceived. "He'd be thirty now, my son," he said. *How strange*, I kept thinking afterward. *He knew the child was male.*

Not every woman to whom I talked had similar feelings. A few said, in so many words, "I'm glad I didn't have a kid. I would have been a horrible mother." But does any woman who gets an abortion think she'd be a great mother? That I thought I would have been a bad mother went without saying. That I assumed I would have been a bad mother—that I was incompetent, that I had no capacity for love, that the guy would bail—was the whole problem: a mindset emblematic of a life based on way too much fear and not nearly enough faith; on way too much craving for anesthesia and not nearly enough hunger for the truth.

Speaking of the truth, I couldn't play both ends from the middle. I couldn't think of the people who believed, say, that the world was created in seven days as pitiful primitives and also, after looking at photos of fetal development, refuse to concede that life begins at conception. One truth transcends all politics, science, commerce, technology, and culture; all peer pressure, ridicule, and scorn; all time, all space, all history. That is the truth of the human heart.

In the human heart, things are not hip, arch, sophisticated, cynical, clever, effective, self-righteous, self-justifying, or convenient. They're either right—which is to say toward love and life in all its forms; or they're wrong, which is to say away from. They're simple and childlike. You don't have to be a theologian to believe that human beings have souls. You don't have to be a metaphysician to feel an instinctive urge to protect life, especially life that is weaker than you. A kid cries at the death of a kitten. A kid will protect a bird's egg.

I'm not talking about sentimentality, which has been defined as giving to a thing more tenderness than God gives to it. Sentimentality is why so much of the discussion about abortion rings false. We don't have any other imagery so we use the image of babies. Then we pretend that babies, for all the joy they (apparently) bring, aren't in another way a giant pain in the ass. We pretend a baby doesn't blow the life of the parents, especially the mother, apart. We pretend babies don't grow into first children, then teenagers, then adults who suffer unbelievably and inflict suffering on others—because suffering is what life, in large part, consists. Not every child is going to be born into an ideal situation. Some people are going to better parents—way better—than others. Some children are going to be more rejoiced over than others. That's the way the world is: messy, awkward, unpredictable, inconsistent and inconvenient. That's reality.

Reality is also the only place where we can hope to find true growth, transcendence, mystery, humor, connection, or joy— which is exactly why sentimentality is so dangerous. The right tends to be sentimental toward babies, and to have no tenderness at all toward the single mothers and the often disenfranchised, troubled, hungry, lonely, uninsured, uneducated children they struggle to raise alone after choosing to bring their pregnancies to term.

The left purports to be tenderer than God by trying to head all such suffering off at the pass. We will save the unwanted child from suffering by destroying it, the thinking goes. We will save the mother from suffering by helping her to take the shortcut. We will save the father—but then we don't have to save the father. The father, as always, can walk away any time he likes. We've never had to save the father. That's one reason both the left and the right miss the mark, and why abortion can never be reduced to politics.

That's also why my blood runs cold whenever I see a guy, purporting to be on the side of women, aggressively supporting abortion. I recently learned that David Foster Wallace, God rest his soul, apparently once made a comment to the effect that his goal as a writer was to teach his readers that they were smarter than they thought they were. *I beg your pardon, I wanted to retort, but I do not need you to teach me how smart I am.*

That's similar to how I feel when men feel moved to support abortion. Don't do me any favors. Please. I don't need you to promote my "rights." I don't need you to condescend, patronize, and purport to have the faintest, slightest idea of what it is to be a woman expecting a child, especially when you stand to get more no-strings-attached sex from the deal than ever. I love men but could anyone, in fact, possibly stand to "gain" more from abortion—in the sense of being let off the hook when they shouldn't be—than men do?

Beneath abortion lies the split between men and women depicted in the story of the Garden of Eden; the rift decreeing that henceforward, we would all be baffled, bewildered, longing to connect; all aching for each other and at the same time afraid of each other. But how, as women, can we possibly expect to heal the split by overprotecting men, by bearing in our bodies, souls, and nervous systems a burden that should be theirs to share, by remaining silent, by pretending that sustaining this almost mortal wound doesn't hurt and doesn't matter, by confusing the private with the secret and furtive?

If abortion is so wonderful, why are we so reluctant to expose it to the light? Why, at the clinic, do all involved use the word "procedure?" Why, when gazing into the bassinet of our friend's newborn baby do we tend not to exclaim: "Adorable!" I aborted mine!" Everyone's on board for the sex, but no-one likes to think of what transpires afterward for the woman who aborts. No long, hot kisses then. No delighted tandem gaze at the ultrasound: *Honey, look at his tiny feet!* Afterward does not bear looking at, thinking about, or in any particular remembering. That's why for so long I had not wanted to know. My mind would go so far and no further.

The fact is you get crucified if you have the kid; you get crucified if you don't. Fire or fire. You either undergo the redemptive suffering of taking responsibility for your actions on the one hand, or the neurotic (because avoidable) suffering of failing to. I don't see any way around this. I don't think there is a way around it. Hence: "I am the Way, the Truth and the Life."

The cross is a picture of the human condition and the human psyche. Jacques Fesch (1920-1957), for example, was a Parisian wastrel who shot a cop, was sentenced to death, and had a conversion experience in prison. "It's only a short time since I really understood what the cross is," he wrote before going to the guillotine. "It is simultaneously miraculous and horrifying. Miraculous, because it gives us life, horrifying because if we do not bring about our own crucifixion, we have no access to life."

That's something you tend not to hear from either the "pro-lifers" or the "pro-choicers"—nor nearly enough, for that matter, in church. I once heard a truly dreadful homily from a priest who told of a baby who'd been "saved" from abortion. Twenty years later, the "baby" was a strapping blond quarterback with a 4.0 at Notre Dame. Nobody would want to take that away from the guy, but why not choose as your pro-life poster child a 20-year-old with Down syndrome, or a flaming drag queen, or an abscessed meth freak? Why not acknowledge that a good percentage of the babies who are "saved" are going to become broken-down homeless people, illegal immigrants, and vicious criminals?

That of course is no reason to promote abortion; in fact, that's the very reason abortion is wrong. Let's remember who we're dealing with here, folks: the unfathomable human race. We're all bothersome. We're all, in our ways, broken. Which somehow makes it all the more imperative that we not lose a single member. We're responsible for each other. We live and die by each other. We need all the help we can get.

That we're saving saints is one false picture of abortion. Another is that the typical abortion-seeker is a nine-year-old victim of rape by her fat, drunken stepfather. In fact, less than 1% of abortions are sought in response to rape or incest (not that even one case of rape or incest is good news). The three major reasons, in fact, seem to be roughly "negative impact on the mother's life," "financial instability," and "relationship problems/unwillingness to be a single mother."

Scrolling through several such lists, I could feel all over again the cold sweat, the terror, the thoughts circling round and round: *Where am I gonna get the money to raise a kid?… Not steady enough on my feet… Don't even bother telling him…*

Where is the guy? Where is ever the guy?…

Maybe that long-ago radio interviewer had been right in saying

I'd taken the easy way, but abortion had also proven to be the lonely way. I took full responsibility for my own choices. But I had also grown up in a family affected by generations of alcoholism in which I had learned at a very young age that displaying feelings, making a mistake, or having needs was dangerous. From the beginning, I'd been over-achieving and hyper-responsible. I'd been a straight-A student who'd won the spelling bee and the talent contest and the American Legion award and the MVP girls' basketball award and still felt like a fraud, a failure, and a fluke.

Also from an early age I'd had a secret, hidden life: the world of books; the call of the introspective, sensitive heart to be a writer. Instead, I graduated from high school and embarked upon what would turn out to be twenty years of hard drinking, one-night stands, the flagrant degradation of the female barfly. In college, I majored in Social Service rather than creative writing, because deep in my heart I wanted to be "good" and I thought that meant "helping" people. I went on to earn a law degree because I wanted to be loved and I thought pursuing a goal of my own would be selfish and pushy.

I got sober in 1987, then embarked upon a fourteen-year marriage through which we had both faithfully soldiered but that had begun with—had centered upon—a death, the abortion of the child we'd conceived together, and that almost inevitably had not lasted. I stayed—seeking and striving and pondering nonetheless; becoming a writer, becoming a Catholic—because I believed marriage was a sacrament; because I abhorred breaking a vow. The divorce was preceded by the slow, cruel death of my father and followed by my being diagnosed with breast cancer.

And then, after I'd worked so hard to not despair, to stay standing, to become awake and joyful and alive and spiritually mature, I'd fallen hopelessly in love—perhaps subconsciously been compelled to fall in love—with someone who didn't, or couldn't, love me back. Everything I had never been able to offer a man before—emotional generosity, a semblance of purity, my passion for food, music, writing, books—I had offered, and my offering had been rejected. I had yearned to create something that was bigger than either of us and my desires had come to a stillbirth. I was past 50 by this time, and that I would die a dry well, having failed at the one thing that mattered on earth, was a grief so extreme that some days I could hardly breathe.

Here's the real secret sorrow of abortion: the desire to get rid of the unborn is also a desire to get rid of the women who get pregnant with them: people who don't fit in, people who don't get it, poor people, unlucky people, people who think if you sleep with the guy he'll love you, people who think sex is the only thing they have to offer, people who hunger and thirst for connection but tend to self-sabotage, people who have difficulty believing that there will be enough: money, support, love.

People who believe there will be enough don't tend to get dolled up on a Saturday night (as I had during "the dark years)," make their way down to the local cesspool bar, and sit there hoping against the hope that at closing time the racist, misogynist bartender will deign to come home with them. People who believe they're worth cherishing don't tend to think that a two-hour talk—no matter how hilariously funny the guy is, no matter that he, too, adores Kafka!— is enough of a bond to immediately jump into bed: especially if he's married. And as for married (or, as I'd been, engaged) women who get abortions: wouldn't two people who really loved each other, who had the kind of partnership we all yearn for, be so committed that they'd be dying to bring a child they'd conceived to term, no matter how much of a stretch?

Here's another truth: when you do something that goes against your deepest soul, you feel guilty. I should have felt guilty. Not the sickly, self-obsessed guilt that worries about being punished, or thinks sex is wrong, but the guilt that came from knowing I'd had an opportunity to walk toward the light and I'd blown it. I'd had an opportunity to help repair the human fabric and I'd torn it asunder.

As the Swiss mystic and philosopher Father Maurice Zundel observed:

> *We are not interchangeable. We cannot put ourselves in someone else's place. Each one of us is unique, irreplaceable, and if human love means anything, it is because it offers the possibility of showing this unique face that we are to someone else. Each soul is unique. If it were not so, it would be terrible. The soul is not some*

kind of mill open to anyone, but it is a secret, a unique mystery
which will never be seen again, indispensable to the world order
and the obliteration of which would disturb the order of the
universe. *

I had disturbed the order of the universe, and I believed that to disturb the order of the universe has eternal consequences. That is the cardinal sin in our culture, the über-unhipness: to believe that our souls are battlegrounds between good and evil. To believe that our actions have eternal consequences.

To believe that our actions have eternal consequences gives rise to feelings not easily resolved by psychotherapy, yoga, or Tarot card readings. I had certainly begun the work over the years— examinations of conscience, inventories of resentments and fears, writing and sharing with another my sexual and emotional history. I'd come a long, long way—toward maturity, toward healing—but mentally and psychically I often still seemed to be in battle. I could be harsh and judgmental, both with others and myself. I often woke from sleep at war with an unseen adversary: subconsciously intent on establishing that I was "right," on defending myself, on proving my innocence. But I could not defend myself. No adequate excuse existed. By any worldly notion of justice I was doomed: a mother who had destroyed, killed if I had to use the word, my own children.

Without grace, the door would remain forever locked. Without mercy, there was no escape. I couldn't hope to move forward unless

I started by asking: *Could I have ever been that misguided, that blind, that astray?* I couldn't hope to progress until I was willing to expose the accumulated pain of a lifetime to the light and ask for help.

So twenty-plus years after the fact, I sought help. I hadn't even been sure help existed, but "post-abortion counseling," as it's known—from secular to Jewish, Christian, New Age, Buddhist and beyond—turned out to be a going concern. Others would find another approach more helpful, but for my part, I could not imagine approaching an issue that impinged so deeply upon my capacity for love, my sexuality, my body, except through Christ—which is to say, through his Church. As Flannery O'Connor observed, the central Christian mystery is that life, "for all its horror, has been found by God to be worth dying for." That mystery was the ground of my existence.

I got in touch with an organization called Project Rachel (affiliated with or under the auspices of the Archdiocese of LA). I made an appointment. Then, one late fall afternoon, I drove to the suburb of Rosemead, parked at the Pregnancy Help Center—a one-story Cape Cod-type house in the middle of a strip mall—and was ushered into an office dominated by an anatomically correct pink plastic sculpture of a womb-enclosed fetus. Here I met with a woman named Christine

Christine was about my age, married with grown children, and she'd been working with people like me for thirty-two years. "Of all the people in the universe," she pointed out that first session, "you're the one to whom your children are most connected."

That notion alone floored me. I'd thought maybe calling the beings I'd conceived "children" was other-worldly and weird. And if they *were* children, I'd considered myself the *last* person on earth worthy to have a relationship with them.

I had also never remotely imagined that I could come to terms with…I decided to just go ahead and call them my children. The very idea made me want to burst into tears, get mad, go off and be by myself. Deep down, I'd never felt myself fully forgiven; couldn't believe I'd been forgiven. I'd felt what I'd done was too big for me to turn to Christ with it. I'd thought even he would turn away his face. But really I had turned my face, or a part of it, away from him. For all my very real spiritual progress, the most tender, most vulnerable part of me had remained closed off, clenched up, ashamed and afraid.

The idea that I could be reunited with these beings I'd conceived, that we could love each other, that together we could form a kind of whole, was so much more than I could have ever dared to hope or believe. I couldn't undo what I'd done. I wasn't proposing to enter into a fairy tale. But if the blind could be made to see, if a paralytic could get up off his mat and walk, if a drunk could get sober, then maybe, unbelievable as the prospect seemed, this wound could at last begin to be healed.

"Begin," I soon learned, was the operative word. I was supposed to try to remember the abortions. I, who remember in almost comically vivid detail sights, sounds, and conversations from decades ago, remembered almost nothing: not the dates, not the faces of the doctors, not what I wore, thought about, ate, felt. I remembered bleakness, coldness, riding home on the subway in Boston alone.

I was to try to undergo the stages of grieving: denial, anger, depression, acceptance. I had to identify and be willing to let go of resentments to which I'd been holding on for decades. If I wanted freedom from bondage, I had to fully release from bondage everyone else I felt had ever done me wrong, including my family, the abortion doctors, the men I'd loved who hadn't quite loved me back the way I'd hoped (understatement!). I had to look at my tendency toward self-justification, my perfectionism, my profound fear of abandonment which—surprise—went back to my own mother.

Over the next several months, I saw the (sainted) Christine (who "charged" on a donation-only basis, by the way) almost every week. I prayed through and with the children. I spoke to them. I made my way through two thick workbooks. I wrote pages and pages—of journal entries, of inventory.

One of my younger brothers during this time "coincidentally" sent me a photo of myself as a child that I'd never seen before. I'd always joked about how I'd (grandiosely) taken it upon myself from a very young age to "save" my family, but this photo shocked me into realizing that I'd come by my illusions honestly. I was standing, alone, in front of the Rhode Island farmhouse in which my mother had been raised. And I saw, as I never had as a kid, that the house was badly, shamefully, in need of repair: dilapidated stoop, derelict shingles, unkempt lawn. A wooden awning sagged over the doorway, behind a half-drawn curtain peeked the ghostly face of my notoriously hermit-like grandmother, and there—as the arrow loaded with eons of unworked-through family baggage was launched—I stood: just shy of my sixth birthday.

Already, little feet firmly planted, hands thrust in coat pockets, I'd been wearing a winning, chin-up, smile. Already, emotional neglect the firm backdrop, my whole pose had said: *Don't worry; I'll be the glue that holds things together!* What generations of sorrow had I inherited? What kind of mothering, when her own mother had gone days without speaking, and her father had vanished one day into thin air, could my poor mother have received? How could she possibly have been expected to pass on more, or other, to me? So much pain was stored in my body and nervous system. Over and over and over again: this has failed. This has died. This effort, longing, love, will not be returned. Somewhere back there I had stopped breathing. I had held my breath once, in an effort to keep the pain at bay, and I had never quite breathed freely again.

I was encouraged me to put names, faces, personality characteristics to the children I'd conceived. Like my friend who'd "known" his aborted child had been male, I instantly knew the first two were girls and the youngest a boy. Here, I was unabashedly influenced by *Whistle Down the Wind*, the 1959 novel by Mary

Hayley Bell in which three children from an English village find an injured, chain-smoking, cryptic, escaped criminal in the barn and think he's Jesus. Which in a sense he is, as we're all Jesus: some—often convicted criminals—more than others. The kids sneak him food and cigarettes, protect him from the grownups, stick with him when the cops come with the bullhorns and baying dogs and guns. They wonder about things. They know not to go to their parents for help. They are realistic, they know about pain, and they also have tender hearts. Their names are Brat (short for Brambling), Swallow, and Poor Baby.

I was supposed to make a collage. You have got to be kidding, I thought. I'm fifty-seven years old and I'm going to cut pictures out of *Cosmo*? I'm in existential crisis here and I'm going to do crafts? Typically, as soon as I started I became obsessively absorbed and spent hours poring through old copies of *The New Yorker*, *Harper's*, *Gourmet*, *Wired*, and *Science*, then gluing my gleanings to a cardboard triptych that, like Dante's *The Divine Comedy*, consisted of Hell, Purgatory, and Paradise.

Hell featured fire, knives, a loan-shark storefront, and a bottle of Gilbey's gin. Purgatory boasted a huge-ass waterfall (for baptism), a picture of a burning bush from a Byzantine fresco, and color-stained photos of the DNA of mouse ears (for the miracle of creation!). For Paradise I'd settled on a Renaissance Madonna and Child from a 1984 Gourmet article on Tuscan food, a girl in a leopard-skin coat jumping rope, and a William Eggleston photo: "Motel, Wildwood,

New Jersey" (I pictured our little family of four leaning mournfully out of separate windows—because they'd be loners, too!—above the eerily spot-lit swimming pool).

The centerpiece consisted of a big blue-green sky full of clouds that were part light, part dark, with way at the top, three tiny, goony baby heads pasted on. Abortion leaves behind no photos, no physical objects to touch or look at or smell, no memories of flesh, nails, hair. A collage was a poor and if you like pathetic facsimile, and it was also the closest I was ever going to come to an incarnation.

The culminating event of treatment was to be a three-day retreat with eight or ten other women. "You're going to love this," Christine had been telling me all along. "What happens over these weekends is unbelievable."

I'm always wary when someone says *You're going to love this*, and sure enough, I arrived Friday night at what turned out to be an aesthetically undistinguished suburban convent. Amy Grant tunes wafted down the hall. Dinner was creamed chicken, canned peas, and a stupendous array of salt-, fat-, and sugar-laden snacks. I was touched to the heart by the generosity of Christine and the other volunteers, but not until I'd snuck off by myself, walked the grounds, and found a prickly pear with salmon-gold blooms, and a hummingbird like a flying sapphire, and the sweet, sweet smell of orange-tree flowers mixed with garbage over by the Dumpster, did I begin to breathe easily.

I would just as soon have been left alone to kvetch, snack, and swap tales with my comrades, but the people in charge, in spite of their almost insane goodwill, had a grueling program on tap which consisted of many group prayers, many songs I would probably not have picked out myself, and a series of role-playing exercises called "Living Scripture."

After hearing the Parable of the Adulterous Woman, for example ("Let him who is without sin cast the first stone"), we each chose one from an array of rocks, which we pledged to carry around for the weekend as a symbol and to put down, in front of the group, when we felt our burden had been lifted.

When are we going to get to process, or pray, or write madly in our journals? I'd already started to wonder by Saturday morning, but I knew enough to "Take what you like and leave the rest." Sacramental life had taught me to overlook any amount of external hokiness and to see the love at the center. The pure intentions of the people who were running the thing, coupled with mine, would stand us all in good stead.

Saturday morning we had more living Scripture, but Saturday afternoon, we were finally invited to break into small groups and share. I am a big, big fan of the shared story. There is some huge transformative power in telling your story, in your own words, not for the purpose of getting critiqued or commented upon or challenged, but simply in order to say: *I am here. I signify.* Also, people tend to be amazingly articulate, sincere, insightful, moving, and with luck, funny, when they're allowed freely to tell their own stories—especially if events are involved of which they are not all that proud.

I nabbed a saucer-sized chocolate chip cookie and settled in. An elderly gal limped in late muttering in an East European accent, "God almighty! Have they changed the schedule again? They change without telling us, no, no, go ahead without me. My life has been hell, HELL!" with a small forbearing smile. This was Karel, 84, who had survived the Nazi occupation of Czechoslovakia, been deported along with her abusive husband to Bolivia, suffered two abortions while awaiting asylum to the U.S. and basically starving to death, and mourned the losses of her children every day for the intervening forty-odd years.

Mai, a Vietnamese bank teller, had aborted after a fling with a Latino gang banger. Narida, an airline executive, had been born in Mumbai, lived all over the world, and undergone five abortions, the last of which, coupled with the dastardly behavior of the guy in question, had prompted a major examination of conscience.

I'd told my own story, or bits and pieces of it, before: in my essays and books, in Confession, to Christine. But to tell it to others who had also suffered abortion was an experience of a different order: a different kind of vulnerability, a different kind of acceptance, a different kind of seeing that, like them, I was a fallible human being who had made some very wrong choices and who had also suffered for them; had perhaps suffered long enough. I didn't tell anything new. I didn't feel any dramatic turning-of-the-corner release. But

I did realize as I spoke that abortion is in a way a kind of suicide. You're killing a part of yourself. You're saying *I'm not worthy to perpetuate my place on earth, my spirit and soul*.

A guy, a young, muscle-bound pipe fitter, was in our group as well. Three years ago he and his girlfriend (who was telling her own story in a separate small group) had agreed to abort the child they'd conceived together. He'd taken her to the clinic that day, and ever since had been devastated. Watching him fidgeting, wringing his hands, groping for the words to describe feelings for which no words exist, I thought: *Now that is a man*. Back with the rest of the retreatants, his girlfriend was the first to speak. Watching her stare down at the floor and say, "I just want him to *love* me again," I thought: How fragile we are, we humans. How much damage we can do.

Lying in bed that night, I saw that the last twenty years had slowly furrowed, watered, prepared the ground for what was happening now, this very weekend. I had committed arguably the worst possible crime against humanity and perhaps I had also had to undergo the worst possible emotional pain in order to be readied for healing. Although perhaps no wound as deep as the wound of abortion ever exactly heals. A wound is accepted and incorporated, just as Christ's wounds were incorporated—not removed, not erased, but incorporated—after the Resurrection.

I had undergone a kind of pruning, a purgation, and in the purgation all of reality had been accepted, and in the acceptance, something new was being made of me. I was both the person who had aborted my children and the lover of Christ; both deeply selfish and deeply giving, both the Virgin Mary and Mary Magdalene—and something more besides. I would continue to stumble, to be broken and weak, to fail. But maybe I could also live out the rest of my life in a way befitting the mother I would like to have been but had not been able to be; the mother I in fact was.

Sunday's schedule featured a gabfest breakfast, then Mass, then preparations for the pièce de résistance "memorial" during which we were to mount the altar, one by one, and pay homage to our unborn child(ren): an event I, for one, was heartily dreading.

I arrived to find the pews stocked with Kleenex and the altar decked with fake flowers. We'd been urged to write a letter to him/her/them, which we were to read out loud, but here I'd balked. For one thing, a letter is between you and the person to whom you write it, so why would I let anyone else in on it? (Plus, sap that I am, I was afraid I'd burst into hyperventilating tears). Besides, my kids would have been in their twenties by now. I didn't think of them as babies, actually. I thought of them as adults with their own joys, problems, likes, dislikes, and massive baggage that any child of mine—especially one I'd aborted—would be likely to have.

So I wormed nervously into a pew, tried to look invisible, and listened to several of the others—grateful, after all, for the Kleenex. Karel's 55-year-old daughter, who had only recently learned of her mother's previous two abortions, had shown up for the service.

Other people had invited siblings, spouses, and friends. My own buddy Yvonne had made the trek from her downtown condo and was lending moral support from a few pews back.

When my turn came, I walked up front, mounted the stairs to the lectern, and said, "This is how I picture my kids."

Fern, my oldest, looks out for the others. Organized, feisty, a scientist of some kind maybe. Deeply smart, sensitive, does not show much but feels keenly. She loves me, but is also, understandably, slightly pissed / hurt and suspicious still as well.

My middle child, a girl, Swallow. Gentle, funny, flies up to her nest in the eaves and ponders. She has books stashed up there and a small store of snacks and refreshes herself, prays, then gathers herself and goes out and is cheerful and has a wry joke and shores people up in a way that doesn't draw attention to itself so that people never know how much she gives away and how deep the cost.

My youngest, a boy, Warren. Lives outside society. In trouble somehow. Worries about his father and me.

I'd meant to read a Wisława Szymborska poem—"Return Baggage"—but instead I looked out over the faces of those women and men with whom I'd been in the trenches all weekend and blurted, "I should have laid down my lives for my children, and instead they laid theirs down for me."

I hadn't meant to say it—I'd never even thought such a thing before—and yet it was true. They had died in a sense so I could live. They had launched, and then accompanied me, on a long, long journey. Without the anguish I had felt on their behalf, I might never have been driven to get sober. Without the keening of my heart, I might never have felt spurred to move to LA, embark on the spiritual path, find my way to Christ, start writing. They had suffered annihilation without a word of reproach and now at long last they had risen up, become visible, appeared, and—in a manner that perhaps couldn't have happened otherwise—I had, too.

And then I stepped down to a receiving line of hugs, a white rose, and a certificate with the kids' names on it saying they were in heaven.

"Hang tough, guys," I whispered to them in the ladies' room after. "Just one more round of 'refreshments,' and then we can bolt."

Nibbling cake topped with lard-laced frosting and exchanging e-mail addresses later, I reflected that hardly a moment of the weekend had jibed with my aesthetic and spiritual "sensibility," but what ever, really, does, unless your own apartment which, let's face it, you can't stay in forever?

"The man of solitude is happy," runs my favorite Thomas Merton line, "but he never has a good time." I hadn't had a good time but I was humbled to the ground by the kindly, self-emptying people who had put the retreat on, I was incoherently grateful, and somehow, somewhere during that weekend, a gigantic burden had lifted.

St. Paul had mercilessly persecuted the early Christians. Dorothy Day had had an abortion and was being considered for canonization. If those two had been forgiven, surely I had been, too. If they'd moved on, surely that was my obligation as well. But first, I had needed to forgive myself. I had needed to be reminded that my fear that there would not be enough had been learned, not willfully, spitefully cultivated. And maybe most of all, I had needed to sit in a circle with other women who had mourned in silence, who had secretly keened, who had had no-one with whom to talk: no support, no exit, no voice.

Heading home, I thought of the cornball things folks tend to mention—first snowfalls, idyllic summer afternoons—in their odes to the kids they didn't have the time or money or hope for. *Not me*, I thought, gazing out over the acres of oddly endearing Southern California dreck: the exhaust-shrouded palm trees, the stray star beginning to burn through the smog. I thought, *I'm sorry they missed this*: the whole weird, inarticulable, excruciatingly painful, exultantly joyful, through-a-glass-darkly experience of life that for all the failure, disappointment, bewilderment, loneliness, and loss, I myself wouldn't have missed for anything in the world.

I was sorry they'd missed all that, but I also couldn't imagine my life any other way than the way it was. I'm not sure I would have had it any other way than the way it was. Even now, I didn't particularly regret not having children. I regretted the violence, the blindness.

I regretted that those particular children hadn't been born. But I also believed I would meet them some day. I had mourned them for twenty years and now I could look them in the eye and tell them I was sorry.

You don't feel bad about things except out of love. They had shown me that I did have a capacity for love. They had reminded me that for all my wrong turns, I had always hungered to draw the world to my breast. They had connected me to the fierce, creatively self-giving life force of all mothers, and all women. They had given me a humble and contrite heart. They had rendered me, finally, worthy of my suffering.

The 10 freeway coming into downtown L.A. can be an extreme sport, especially after dark: the taillights red in the inky night, the silhouette of County Hospital looming to the north, the way I'd lived here so long I knew to merge left before the 710 came up, to stay in the right lane after the hair-pin curve and zip by the backed-up traffic waiting to get onto the 5, to move a couple of lanes left again, as the "Exit Only" lane for the 110 loomed.

Semis barreled by. A lane-cutting motorcyclist nearly nicked my fender. I wondered, as I often do while driving the freeways, if I'd emerge alive, then swerved onto the Vermont/Hoover bypass, cut across four lanes of traffic, and exited at Normandie: one more time, almost home; one more time, safe.

The air smelled of oleanders and frying meat. Streetlamps cast haloes of sallow light on the folks ranged up and down the block like characters in a 21st-century Passion Play.

A panhandler held a sign saying "Trying to Get Back to Tulsa." A man in a wheelchair hawked mangoes from the tailgate of a battered truck. A tattooed teenaged girl, heavily pregnant, peered hopefully up the street for the bus.

My brothers and sisters. My daughters! My sons!

"O felix culpa," we sing each year at the Easter Vigil—the night Christ was resurrected. "O happy fault that merited such and so great a Redeemer."

THE HOLY FAMILY

"You must praise the mutilated world."

—ADAM ZAGAJEWSKI

PRAISE THE MUTILATED WORLD

I'm sometimes asked why I don't become an oblate or tertiary or consecrate my life in some way. Why don't I join a lay movement, people inquire, or a religious community?

The very thought makes me shudder. I am so, so not built for community of any kind, not apparently marriage, and not any other kind of community that lives, eats, and plans together. Oh God, no. I revere parents, tenders of the sick, and shelterers of the poor, for example, but I could never live their lives. I have no capacity whatsoever for chaos, noise, clutter. Just knowing I'm going to be interrupted at 3 p.m. by the guy from UPS can queer my whole morning. I no longer consider these characteristics limitations. They're simply part of who and how I am.

That I'm not built to live in community doesn't mean I don't have a community—in fact, several of them. First and foremost is the fellowship of recovering men and women with whom I've cast my lot for the past thirty-one years. A day doesn't go by but that I don't have a long conversation, celebrate a birthday, ask for or receive guidance, exchange news, sit down over coffee, share a meal, a story or a laugh. I'm on call more or less 24/7. My time is subject to constant interruptions.

My family is another community.

I also have a wide spectrum of people, from all over the world, who come to me for solace, guidance, consolation. They email, they call, they want to visit when they come through town. They hear me speak and they want to have a one-on-one conversation. I feel a deep sense of responsibility not just to respond as best I can, but to live in a way that equips me to respond most fully.

That alone holds me to a standard at least as high as any community would. I don't choose who or how I serve. I have spiritual directors and guides. My life is deeply private, but I have no secrets that I know of—no compulsion or wound or sin or dereliction of duty or conflict that at least one other person doesn't know about. My obedience is to the Church and her teachings—that is, to Christ—rather than to any one community within or outside the Church.

We're called to overlook so much in the Church, so much that is seemingly lacking. At the same time, a priest friend told me the wonderful phrase: *Ecclesia supplet*. The Church supplies: what is lacking in us, in each other, and even in itself. While individually we are full of faults, I find the Church, in her completeness, supplies all my needs.

I've also found the Church is not here to reflect well on me; rather, I'm here to reflect well upon the Church. I've had to give up all idea of propping up my self-image as a follower of Christ by being especially cool, especially weird, especially damaged on the one hand, or especially holy on the other. I've given up all hope of the Church being in any particular the way I want it to be, all hope of the Church's jiving with my aesthetic sensibility, all hope of feeling like I belong, even.

I want to belong; I'm happy to belong. But I don't seek out organizations or movements within the Church of any kind. I've seen too many members of various lay movements come to serve the founder of the lay movement rather than Christ. And after an hour of conversation with Catholic literary folk, nourishing as that can sometimes be, I want to say, "Okay, but why aren't we writing?"

I've also had to learn not to argue or complain, or at least not to try to make a name for myself out of arguing and complaining. To follow Christ is a frightful, ongoing Crucifixion. To identify ourselves with him alone is a scandal, a poverty. Look what they did to our Savior! We can expect the same treatment. Of course we're given many incredible moments of truly meeting people where they are and joy and fun. But it is an exile. Christ never said it wouldn't be.

There are many kinds of exile. One of them, for me, is that since my marriage ended in divorce and annulment around 2000 I've been single. Celibacy, I've learned, is in no way a suppression or ignoring or diminishing of the glory of the erotic urge. Celibacy is an active, ever-evolving state of life, a kind of fourth dimension I've been invited to enter into, interact with, come alive through. Celibacy, in all its fullness, is to my mind one of the highest forms of activism: a way literally to lay down my life for my friends.

I see a straight and unbroken line between my celibacy, for example, and the diminishment of abortion, human trafficking, the porn industry, and all the other hideous ways that the glory of womanhood is degraded and distorted throughout the world. I am firmly convinced that our fidelity to the teachings of the Church somehow saves, say, a young girl in Iraq from a servile marriage, or a woman out alone at night from being raped, or a mother from being beaten by an abusive boyfriend. Only Christ could arrange for such poverty—of companionship, social prestige, financial security—to generate such untold (and to us, invisible) riches. That is the Mystical Body in action.

Even those of us who are weak, older, in my case physically cowardly, are offered the chance to offer up our very bodies for our friends, our fellow women, and our fellow men simply by being faithful to the teachings of the Church. Of course that means far, far more than simply refraining from sex outside marriage. It means, for example, taking constant action, and constantly praying, to be relieved of anger, self-pity, jealousy, lust, and vengeful thoughts.

With all that, celibacy, like marriage, entails a mutilation of sorts. It's the last state that, at the beginning of my pilgrimage, I would have voluntarily chosen. But as Christ said, "The kingdom of heaven is like yeast that a woman took and mixed with three measures of wheat flour until the whole batch was leavened" [Matthew 13:33]. Celibacy for me has been like yeast: a cross, yes but also a mystery and a gift that permeates every area of my existence. It's a radical poverty, and like all forms of true poverty, not one that lends itself to boasting or self-promotion.

In Letters to a Young Poet, Rilke speaks of the solitary life as a calling and a vocation. :

> And perhaps the sexes are more related than we think, and the great renewal of the world will perhaps consist in this, that man and maid, freed from all false feelings and reluctances, will seek each other not as opposites, but as brother and sister, as neighbors, and will come together as human beings, in order simply, seriously and patiently to bear in common the difficult sex that has been laid upon them. *

There's the appalling, crucifying paradox: we become a world to ourselves for the sake of the freedom of the other; of the world.

Out of love, we are called to descend deeper into the solitude we so desperately want to escape. Of course Rilke himself basically abandoned his wife and daughter, lived most of his writing life off the fat of a series of wealthy and adoring female patrons, and by all accounts was almost utterly incapable of forming a true partnership with another human being, woman or man.

Still, he was right. Plus I may not be capable of forming a true partnership—at least not a romantic one—with another human being, either! So be it. Let my prayer be for my unhealthy human attachments to be removed. Let my prayer be to accept my mutilated, still-standing self.

❦ WHEN IN ROME, WALK THE TIBER

Single, childless, in October, 2015, I went to Rome for the Synod on the Family.

My model was Dorothy Day, co-founder of the lay Catholic Worker movement, about whom Russian émigré, fellow convert, and spiritual writer Catherine Doherty observed:

> *An incident from the life of Dorothy expresses well what I am trying to say here. Dorothy went to Rome during the Second Vatican Council. Several years later when I met her in Rome I*

asked her what she did during the time the Council was in session.
She said she had simply taken a room in the poor quarter of the
city, and for ten days she fasted on bread and water and prayed for
the Council. That was all she did! Then she returned to New York
the way she had come—on a freight boat! *

It wasn't exactly like that for me. I rented an Airbnb studio in Campo de' Fiori.

But in my way, I fasted. I ate simply: yogurt, pizza, fruit. I walked everywhere: to the Vatican, to the Villa Borghese, to the train station for a day trip to Assisi. Besides a dinner out and a few coffee dates and tours, I more or less kept silence.

I had a hard time hooking up the splendor of St. Peter's with the Son of Man who rode into Jerusalem on a donkey, whose mother was illiterate, whose father worked with his hands.

I preferred descending on ancient stone steps below street level and walking along the banks of the mostly-deserted Tiber.

While I walked, I pondered.

I thought of how Dorothy Day had given up the love of her life, an atheist who objected to the baptism of the daughter they'd conceived together. She laid down her life for the poor, the marginalized, the hungry. She remained celibate for the rest of her life.

I pondered how a priest friend had recently mentioned that the word mother comes from the same root as matter. Mater Dei: Mother of God. Women, mothers all, we constitute the very matter of God.

I thought of how women are made to nurture, made for relationship. I thought of how the essence of women is that we have the astonishing, miraculous, stupendous, sublime capacity to bring new life into the world. It's our crowning glory. It's not our only glory, but it's our crowning glory.

That's where the women's movement went wrong. Instead of emphasizing the crazy miracle of this ability to bring new life into the world, we diminished it. Like the power-hungry men we purported to despise, we ourselves put the emphasis on the demand to work more, to receive equal pay, to have more worldly power.

We neglected the psychological, emotional, and spiritual aspects of womanhood, to our deep peril. Consequently, we've become ever more marginalized, more overworked, more objectified, and more bullied by our fellow women into toeing the so-called enlightened party line: that men are to blame for all our ills, that sex is meant to be or can be divorced from emotion, that we're entitled to a life without ambiguity, uncertainty or suffering.

The antidote to any lie, including cultural lies, is the truth.

Here's the truth: Men and women are very different. For one main thing, the second a woman has sexual contact with a man, no matter how inappropriate, substandard, or ill-suited he may be, she becomes emotionally attached. You can argue with that fact, say the fact is imbecilic, try to tweak the fact out of existence, but the fact remains.

That's why the seduction scene in the Flannery O'Connor short story "Good Country People" to my mind trumps every piece of "feminist" agitprop ever written.

Hulga, the story's protagonist, is a surly intellectual—and a virgin—with a wooden leg. Home to her country people from college, and incensed by the stupidity of her mother and backward neighbors, she decides to seduce a traveling Bible salesman. As the two climb to the hayloft of her mother's barn, Hulga shrewdly assesses the way she's going to get this bumpkin to sleep with her, then dump him.

He sweet-talks her into allowing him to remove her wooden leg—an ugly thing in a flat brown shoe of which she is nonetheless as proud and protective as a peacock (as we are of our vulnerabilities).

Two seconds after they kiss, she's visualizing the two of them spending their lives together.

After which the Bible salesman—one of the "simple" folk Hulga so despises—opens his suitcase to reveal a stash of booze, porn, and condoms. "You ain't so smart," he snarls, "I been believing in nothing since the day I was born."

Then he disappears down the ladder, making off with her wooden leg and leaving her stranded in the hayloft.

If you make even the smallest deal with the devil, in other words, you'd better be prepared to suffer the consequences.

Yet where in contemporary literature is the story where, out of a higher love, a couple refuses to enter into such a deal? Where is the complex, difficult, beautifully written,-acted and produced film where two people who are attracted to each other (or even one of them) voluntarily abstain?

To refrain from instantly jumping into bed whenever the urge arises is literally beyond the ken of our cultural imagination. The loneliness and emptiness of no-strings-attached sex is instead accepted silently, stoically, without comment, as proof of our liberality and open-mindedness.

In a 2015 *New Yorker* profile of Gloria Steinem, for example, a fellow feminist who'd recently returned from Amsterdam reported to her that Dutch sex workers despise the good-will efforts of the West to wipe out human trafficking. "We like our jobs," she insisted. "We're free."

Gloria allowed as how she didn't see how any woman would choose, as her first, best option, to be a prostitute.

But why not? Steinem herself proudly touts the many lovers she's had over the years: some casual, some longer-lasting. These include the real-estate developer and publisher Mort Zuckerman, Franklin Thomas, former head of the Ford Foundation, the "great alto saxophonist and composer" Paul Desmond, the director Mike Nichols, and the Ford Administration's Assistant Attorney General for Civil Rights, Stan Pottinger. From her two-story Upper East Side brownstone, she loves "great sex," which is what we call it when we're rich enough that we don't need to get paid for it.

The woman who is poor enjoys no such luxury as "great sex."

The woman who is poor is trying to feed the children she conceived during what was probably mediocre to bad sex, if you want to rate it.

The point being that the personal *is* political, as we were so found of spouting in the '60s and '70s. What we do in private helps create a culture whose standards are imposed on those who are often least able to bear them.

The fact is we're always either moving toward rigorous honesty, consistent reasoning, and an ongoing examination of conscience, or we're moving away from it, taking the shortcut, living a lie.

Our actions and our reasoning are either going toward the degradation and oppression of women, or away from it; toward cherishing and protecting all that is most precious in all women, or toward offering what should be most inviolable in us up for grabs.

A guy friend recently purported to be in favor of women's "reproductive rights." "It's her body," he insisted. "She should have an abortion if she wants one." I refrained from saying, "If you're so down with women, why don't you quit watching porn?"

Men who equate abortion with freedom, in other words, also very logically tend to be for the "freedom" of women to be sex workers, prostitutes and porn stars. And again, why not? Could anything delight an unwilling-to-commit guy more than having sex with a woman who's saying, "I *want* to be a prostitute?" Could anything make it easier for a guy to bolt or betray than putting all the responsibility for an unplanned pregnancy on the woman?

If men were really "for" women, they'd either firmly commit

before having sex or, if the woman got pregnant, stick around and commit to helping to raise and support a family.

Such old-school righteousness, responsibility, manliness, and gallantry are, again, almost beyond our cultural ken. We women no longer dare hope for such traits, if we ever did, but why? If we're so "strong," why haven't we asked for, insisted upon, and done everything in our power to foster them?

The inability or refusal to see the consequences of our actions is astounding. Because who, one more time, gets the short end of the "reproductive rights" stick? Women, who more than ever willingly work toward the degradation, bondage and objectification of ourselves and our sisters throughout the world.

"Then every scribe who has been instructed in the kingdom of heaven is like the head of a household who brings from his storeroom both the new and the old," said Christ. [Matthew 13:52]. If the "old" is women's capacity to bear life into the world, the "new" consists in the civil rights we've won. Instead of using them to examine the systems—consumerism, militarism, nationalism, for example—to which we're way more deeply in bondage than paternalism, the bondage continues.

In fact, I'm not sure it was lack of rights that drove all those repressed 50's housewives to the brink so much as it was capitalism: the desperate attempt to maintain a controlled and perfect image in the eyes of our peers, including our fellow women. Part of the human condition, and especially of American culture, is our deep-seated fear of being thought losers, of being poor in any way.

That's what makes the family seem a burden rather than a joy. That's why we so desperately want to control: because the family costs, in every way.

⁓

I'm perfectly capable of developing my own itinerary. But in Rome, I more or less went where other people wanted me to.

"If you have a chance, could you go to Santa Maria Sopra Minerva and say a prayer for me?" (This, from a husband and father of five who does not pretend parenthood a picnic). From a seminarian: "Could you light a candle for me at St. Augustine's, that I stay faithful to my vows?" "Could you say a prayer for my 82-year-old mother who's still having difficulty adjusting to being a widow?" "If you get to St. Peter's, please say a prayer for my work before the tomb of Pope John XXIII." "Don't miss the Basilica of San Clemente. Could you pray for the repose of my mother's soul in the apse?"

In some very small, very tenuous, very unremarkable way, in other words, my time in Rome was oriented toward others, toward service, toward the human family.

That is my life.

⁓

In some ways St. Peter's, as I said, was hard to take. The paramilitary-trained Swiss guards wearing the sword that Christ, on his way to Calvary, told Peter to put aside. An altar that's supposedly taller than the Statue of Liberty, designed by the sculptor Bernini, who had an affair with his assistant's mistress, and when he discovered that the mistress was sleeping with his own brother, threatened to slash her face. After which *she* was jailed for adultery.

Still, a patriarchal Church would have as its most enduring, reverenced emblem a father possessively admonishing a daughter, or a father instructing his son in the art of warfare.

Instead, the Church gives us a Mother: nurturing, sheltering, sorrowing over a Son.

In a niche at St. Peter's resides Michelangelo's Pietà. Even the hordes of selfie-stick wielding fellow pilgrims couldn't cloud the stupendous, heart-stopping beauty of this sculpture before which I first gasped, then stood rooted in silence, and at last wept. The seminarian who was giving me a tour pointed out that Christ is almost falling off Mary's lap. It's as if she's delivering him to the altar from which he will feed the world.

No matter our age, socioeconomic status, or station, we are called to order our lives to the human family. If we're single, we are called lay down our lives for other people's children.

In *Life of Jesus*, French novelist François Mauriac observed:

> *The Son of Man did not solve all the sad problems of sex. For*
> *those who wish to follow him, he did not solve the question, he*
> *suppressed it. That the friends of Christ carry their inclinations*

from birth, that they are subject to the weight of this or that heredity, all this he ignores. He requires that they sit down to meager fare, that they refuse to slake all thirst outside marriage. Scandal of scandals in the eyes of the pagan, crime against nature, the diminishing of manhood. But as for him, he cared nothing for the approval of the world. 'Not for the world do I pray...' The Son of Man knew that it is by purity we go to him, and that the flesh shelters the possibility of delights which, here satisfied, give to the creature the illusion of infinite pleasure——in other words that the flesh is his rival. He was indignant to see the Apostles harshly rebuff the children who were jostling about him. In them at least, lust was not yet awakened.

Unbelievable demand! To enter the Kingdom one must become a child again, be a little child. 'Whosoever shall not receive the kingdom of God like a little child shall never enter it!' *

Like Mary, we're called to hold the tension of creation to the breaking point, to resist to the last drop of blood becoming a commodity, a statistic, an algorithm in the service of the crushing worldly kingdom that worships money, power, control, and prestige.

"Pietà" means compassion, mercy. "Virgin" means at-one-with herself.

 THE PARADISE OF SEXUAL REVOLUTION

"Visit a prison and ask the men in the cell blocks to recount their sexual histories, and those of their mothers and fathers. Visit a hospital, and see the faces of women who have determined to violate their inmost natures as the givers of life. Visit a neighborhood—if you can find one; for your paradise has placed transience and infidelity at the heart of the most intimate of human relations."*

—Anthony Esolen, from "The Paradise of Sexual Revolution"

The stage set for the greatest story ever told begins when the star rises in the East over the Holy Family.

The teachings of the Church on sex don't separate me from that family, as promiscuity during my drinking years did: they allow me, and everyone else, to participate. They invite us all to contribute: our talents, our brokenness. They invite everyone to sit at the table around which the Holy Family, which is to say the human family, is gathered: all those who for whatever reason cannot, or are not moved to, raise a family; the old, the unattractive, the disabled and poor; the misfits and malcontents and die-hard solitaries, the temperamentally unsuited and vocationally unavailable; the sexually, emotionally and physically damaged, wounded, and disordered.

Because we are all disordered, in our ways, and we are all responsible for what we do as adults, and we all fail in our duty to the children of the world. We all want the person with whom our children come in contact to be pure, but we don't want to be pure ourselves. We want the priest to be pure, and we want to be free to plaster our city streets with billboards of soft-core porn gay women getting it on in Guess bras.

The guy who is always trying to get you into bed is often also the first one who will tell you he screens his daughter's dates and if anything ever happened to her, he'd kill the guy. I'm someone's daughter, too. We're all someone's daughter or son. So the teachings of the Church are beautifully reflective of the fact that everybody— married, single, straight, gay, young, old—has a part to play. Everyone is invited to welcome, rejoice in, marvel at, and support new life and all life. Everyone is invited to contribute toward the healing of the festering sexual wound at the heart of mankind.

I don't think priests become pedophiles because the teachings of the Church are repressive; the Church, and this is not to minimize the horror, hardly has a corner on the sexual abuse of children or any other kind of sexual misconduct/pathology.

I think they become pedophiles because they are dying for love, for connection, and they have deep psycho-sexual-emotional-spiritual wounds, and I think the reason this seems and in fact is so monstrous, such a hideous betrayal of innocence and trust, is that for it to take place within the context of the Church, of faith, falls so far short of Christ; is so egregious a betrayal.

"What father among you would hand his son a snake when he asks for fish? Or hand him a scorpion when he asks for an egg?" [Luke 11:11-12].

To abuse a child is to give him a scorpion.

For a priest to molest a child is an unimaginable violation, on every possible human level. So as a member of the Church you hang your head in sorrow, in shame, in grief; you feel utter compassion for the child, and I think you also have to feel utter compassion for the priest, and then you ask: How can I help? How can I be part of the solution? How can I not finger-point, but in a sense do penance?

I have pondered this deeply, and at length, and have come to conclude that I can't be sleeping around, and watching porn, and using people as objects, sexually or otherwise, and claim to be any much better than a pedophile priest. And at any rate, if I am doing those things, I am certainly not helping. Each of our actions is always moving either toward or away from helping the pedophile priest, and the children he's molesting or may molest in the future.

For some reason I'm thinking of a recent Saturday afternoon. I was in church for the vigil Mass, and before Mass, I went to Confession.

There was a bit of a line. I've always felt humbled among people who are trying to grapple, however inarticulately, with the state of their souls. Still, waiting my turn, hungry, lonely, tired, and a little angry, I was thinking as usual, *So big deal, I'm a gossip and tend to hate everyone who's not just like me, I bet a lot of other people are worse, plus can "impure" thoughts and acts really be sins especially when I am nervous, high-strung, fearful, emotionally overwrought, and close to perishing from loneliness? And really like sex? Think sex is a good, warm, nourishing, life-enhancing, holy, transcendent thing!*

In one way my sexual "sins" were the least of what weighed on my soul, but the tendency toward fantasy, greed, lust, possession, jealousy, envy, desire to control, and objectification that permeated all parts of my life weren't. I do periodically like to acknowledge my brokenness in this area, and the other ways I'm broken, and to ask for God's blessing and help.

So Confession was good.

And Mass was good.

And walking home afterward, I ran across a kid who was practicing on his skateboard. He'd found a mangy strip of sidewalk, this kid, and he was completely absorbed with this skateboard. He did a run, teetering a bit, but he stayed on the board, and when he hit a bump, he made a small tentative jump. As soon as he got to the end of his strip, he hopped off, turned the board around, and proceeded to start in the other direction.

You could just tell he'd been up and down this little section of sidewalk a hundred times that day: determined, absorbed, dreaming. He had a beautiful face, he'd grow up and break hearts, but right now he was maybe 10, a kid with a mission: learning to skate. It was just one of those moments you can't plan for, that happen so fast, but you know, I got a little pang. This kid on his skateboard, none of us are here forever, life will continue after we're gone, and may there always be a springtime and a kid in a T-shirt and his hair hanging in his eyes learning to skate.

So I smiled at this kid and ceded the sidewalk and he smiled back and a hundred yards or so on, I stopped dead in my tracks. Because I suddenly realized that I was in total solidarity with this kid. There was no separation. I had a life that was private, as we all do and should, but I did not have a life that was secret, that I felt conflicted about, that I had a reason to hide from the world.

I had the experience of an adult, an adult who'd taken many wrong turns along the way, but I was also in total solidarity with this kid because my heart and my body, insofar as possible, were pure.

I didn't know him but I was doing everything in my power to make the world a safe, beautiful, interesting place for him, and every other kid, to grow up in. I used to pass kids on the street and I'd think, *Enjoy it while you can, baby, because there is HELL in store*. I'd think, *You have NO IDEA*. I'd think, *Oh the world is a cruel, harsh place*.

In one way it is harsh and cruel, but mainly because we make it that way. I'm not talking about innocence. I am far, far from innocent, and by ten, a kid isn't innocent either. A kid of ten knows all about good and evil, about suffering, about loneliness. A kid of ten totally knows the score.

But you can know the score and still be lost in wonder. You can know the score and still want to devote a few thousand hours to learning how to skateboard or watch birds or write—in fact, that you do know the score is exactly why you want to do those things. Because you know those things are an antidote somehow. Those things are your turf, the ground you stake out, your way of saying, *I will not be defeated. I will not hold back. I will not be afraid to fail, trip, stumble, lose my way, fall. I will give everything I have to the world, to God.*

I wasn't innocent. But I could rejoice at and feel in solidarity with this kid because I had the heart of a child. The Church had given me back the heart of a child.

If you're looking for what you can get, the teachings of the Church don't make any sense at all.

But if you're longing to give all you have, they're the *only* thing that makes sense.

🖋 OUR CATACLYSMIC, LIFE-GIVING YES

I once attended a Mass at which the clearly deeply disordered priest spent his whole homily taking the congregation, in particular young, beautiful girls, to task. They should hide their knees! Do they want to be instruments of the devil!

As soon as young people kiss, this priest tells them, they must never *ever* see or talk to that person again because they have wrecked their chances for putting God first.

He used his whole homily to complain, carp, and look down upon all the parents with spoiled, ill-behaved children who they, the parents, refuse to properly discipline, the result being that, unlike the children of a couple he knows, these spoiled, corrupt young wastrels will not grow up to have their very first kiss at the altar.

I understood what the priest was trying to get at. The early and over-sexualization of kids who are way too young to know better is enough to make anyone want to start battening down the hatches.

But as the writer Madeleine L'Engle once observed, "We do not draw people to Christ by loudly discrediting what they believe, by telling them how wrong they are and how right we are, but by showing them a light that is so lovely that they want with all their hearts to know the source of it." *

This priest's whole homily, by contrast, was about saying no—no, no, no, no without in any way explaining that the reason for all those noes is a larger, sublime yes.

Contemplative monk Erasmo Leiva-Merikakis (now known as Brother Simeon) wrote: "Léon Bloy…once said that if we receive the Eucharist and fail to practice charity, fail to allow the Eucharist to have in us the effects that by its very nature it must have, then 'the sacred Host we have consumed, rather than nourishing us, will become within us like a bomb exploding our hypocrisy to high heaven.' " *

Catholicism does not consist in some timid, rigid, dead set of rules. Catholicism is our hearts, our bowels, our erotic energy, our lives! The whole purpose of the rules is to allow us to explode within them. To follow Christ, to be Catholic, to practice chastity in the deepest sense of the word is to hold an almost unbearable amount of tension in our bodies, spirits, and nervous systems— which paradoxically allows us to break out in all kinds of other sublimely interesting, glorious directions and ways.

Look at Thérèse of Lisieux, one of the Church's most well-know, well-loved saints. In *The Story of a Soul*, she admits that if she'd ever fallen for a guy, she would have been worse than Mary Magdalene. She wrote the Apostle's Creed in blood on a piece of paper she then wore under her habit, against her heart. She formally offered herself to Christ as a Holocaust Victim of Love!

Look at the sky-jabbing spires of Gaudi's masterpiece church, the Sagrada Familia.

Look at the Gerard Manley Hopkins poem "Pied Beauty." That— "Praise him" at the end is an ejaculation (from the Latin "darted out;" an old-school Catholic term for a short, pithy prayer), preceded, no less, by the generative thrust of "fathers forth." The poem is all the more sublime for having been written by a gay man—a Jesuit priest and a severe depressive who stayed faithful to his vows and offered his suffering, his loneliness, his love, his failure as a teacher; his body, blood, genius and soul to Christ.

As writer Alice McDermott notes, "Being a Catholic is an act of rebellion. A mad, stubborn, outrageous, nonsensical refusal to be comforted by anything less than the glorious impossibility of the resurrection of the body and life everlasting." *

The reason to hold on until the altar, in other words, is not because you are so listless and etiolated and body-despising and intent on being a straight-A Catholic that you'll suppress and deny your own God-given erotic urge. The reason to hold out is because you are so vital, so wild with longing, so crazy about your spouse-to-be that you want to make your wedding night a work of art. You want to offer your wedding night to the whole world.

So what that priest forgot to add is, "Man, and let's hope that couple who waited till their honeymoon had the night of their lives! Let's hope those two saw stars! Maybe they conceived a kid and if so, let's hope that kid is juiced to the skies with life, with enthusiasm, with poetry and song and jokes, with the capacity to suffer and the capacity to love."

That is the opposite of no, no, no. That is one cataclysmic, self-giving, aching, life-affirming yes.

POET RITA A. SIMMONDS
ON THE SACRAMENT OF MARRIAGE

Rita is a friend, an award-winning poet, a wife, and a mother. We met in the mid-aughts in New York.

We've had many discussions since. Wandering the streets of Los Feliz in the summer of 2012, I spoke to her via phone of her marriage. With her permission, I taped the conversation. Here's the transcript.

Me: Let's just chat. I'm thinking I'll run this on my blog August 28th because that was my parent's wedding anniversary and it's also the memorial of St. Augustine. Whose right eye offended him and he more or less plucked it out: love, lust, the holy longing. A good day to write of marriage.

Rita: August 28th is also the day of Frank's surgery.

Oh good, we'll think of him…Okay so the very first thing: you have to tell us about is when you had a nervous breakdown and Mother Teresa kicked you out of the Missionaries of Charity.

She didn't kick me out. What happened was I joined right out of college.

And you're a total cradle Catholic?

Yes, and I always believed. And I was always very ambitious spiritually. Very interested in my salvation. I saw there were temptations out there trying to sidetrack me but I always knew my purpose in life was to serve Him. That was always very, very clear. At that time Mother Teresa was really the person who was out there, besides Pope John Paul II. She was really the one to watch, she was the one to follow, the one who caught everyone's attention, especially those who were trying to follow the Church, to follow Christ. So I met up with the Sisters in the South Bronx, I was working at their summer camp. I met with Sr. Priscilla, who was the Regional Superior at the time. She invited me to do what they call a come-and-see, so I went and I was really taken with their life, and I loved it. I loved the prayer and I loved the total gift of self, that you would give every aspect of your life, all centered around Christ. Every gesture. We would wake up in the morning and we would say prayers as we put on our clothes. It was just amazing. The bell would ring; the bell was the voice of God. Chapel, whatever it was you had to do. I loved it, I really loved it for about the first year, and then it started getting really difficult.

What got difficult about it?

Um . . . it just became very . . . I didn't know how to express myself in that climate any more. [Laughing] It's a very austere life. The one thing Sr. Frederick who ended up becoming the regional Superior, she said, "Sister,

I think you need to serve God in freedom." Instead of confined to that very disciplined lifestyle.

When you say austere, what do you mean? The food? The schedule?

You never sit on a couch, for example.

What do you sit on?

Benches, the floor. In the chapel, you sit on the floor. You wake up at 4:40 in the morning. You clean the floor every single day, you sweep and swab the floor. I don't know about you, but I never wash my floor every single day.

I don't even wash mine every month. Did they yell at you for laughing?

You can laugh in recreation, a lot, but I did get in trouble for breaking silence. I had another woman in there at the same time, she was actually the only woman in my postulant group who moved on to the novitiate, and we used to crack each other up all the time and you weren't supposed to be laughing in the stairwell...It was hard...I wasn't really able to be formed there. I just didn't really fit in after a while.

So what happened?

Toward the end when things were getting really bad...first of all, I hate to cook, I've always hated cooking. I've never been a good cook, I've never enjoyed it. I had the responsibility of cooking lunch for all the sisters who were at the house on retreat. There were many, many sisters. So I had to make rice for them. And there were two different ways to make it and I wasn't sure if I should...I didn't know...I just didn't know what I was doing, basically, and so I made a huge mess of the whole lunch. It was like ten minutes before the bell was going to ring for the Angelus and one of the professed sisters came downstairs to see how I was progressing and...I just told her that lunch wasn't anywhere near ready, that basically I didn't know what I was doing. So she said, "Well here, open this can of tomatoes." So I went to open the can of tomatoes and it splattered all over my white sari. And I just broke down.

Ohhhh...

I ran upstairs and into the bathroom and I locked myself in the bathroom and I would not come out. I just couldn't do it anymore.

Think of the symbolism of the red and the white!...

That experience meant so much to me, was so precious to me, being with the Sisters, still to this day. Talking about Mother Teresa is like talking about my mother. She was really my spiritual mother.

So you met her?

Oh yes, I met her. I spoke to her a couple of times. I saw her privately twice.

And she was holy, right?

Oh yes. She was very small. She looked dead in your eye. She didn't waste words. And she wanted to know who her sisters were and I think she was looking at me like, "Is this young woman suited to this life?" I really think she was looking at me and trying to help me. She had to do that. Her initial calling was among the Indian sisters. For an American to become part of that order is more difficult than for an Indian.

So you were in the bathroom and then what?

I was very nervous. I was afraid. I was shaking uncontrollably. I started having crazy thoughts about my eternal salvation, that I was going to go to hell. I mean this is not me, to have thoughts like that. So I was obviously under some kind of duress. I just remember in the days afterward not wanting to go down to the chapel because I was crying too much and I had to go and I'd just cry, cry, cry. So it was very obvious to everyone that something was wrong with me. Also right around that time we were supposed to write a letter to Mother asking to go to the novitiate. I thought, Maybe if I go to the novitiate things will get better. And Mother wrote back and said, "I'm giving you six more months as a postulant." And I thought, Oh no. I'll never survive here six more months. And I just remember praying about it, and it was the first snowfall of the year, I remember seeing the kids outside the chapel window and they were frolicking in the snow and I just remember thinking, Oh I just want to do that. I just want to play in the snow. And so right then I was called in to speak to Sr. Frederick. And she said, "What do you want to do?" And I said, "Sister, I think I want to leave." And Sister said, "I think so, too."

And that was it.

I even went back later and tried to speak to Sister. I was trying to make it in the world on my own and I really missed that life and I would go back to her and she'd say, "No, you can't come back unless you realize somehow that you made a mistake. That you could have done something differently and you didn't." And I said, "Well I can't say that because I tried as hard as I possibly could. "So…

So from there you went?…

To my mother's, my family, my mom and dad in upstate New York. My mother was devastated. I looked terrible.

How old were you at that point?

Twenty-two.

So you had this whole plan that you were going to be a religious and now you had your whole life ahead of you and you didn't know what you're going to do with it, sort of.

Yeah, I had no idea. My mother said, "I want you to stay home for a month. You need to rest." So I did. But I was counting the days.

And you had how many brothers and sisters?

Um. Five brothers and four sisters.

Okay. And not a ton of money growing up, right?

No, not a lot of money. We always prayed the Rosary. We went to Mass on Sundays and Holy Days. My mother and father both taught us about our faith. And lived it.

And then you met Frank?

No! I didn't meet Frank till I was in my late thirties.

Oh, okay, so fast forward then and tell us what you did in the intervening years till you met Frank.

Well I had a friend in college and we'd formed a pro-life club at Hofstra University. We'd become very good friends. So after my month at home I went to NYC to be close to my friends. And my friend Rich, who is now Fr. Rich, invited me to this group that was meeting at St. Patrick's Cathedral at the time that was called Communion and Liberation. Basically from that time on I was very involved, still am involved, with CL.

Which is a lay movement?

Yes, and that's where I was all those years. 1988 on. I hoped that I could…since I'd tried to become a nun and couldn't, I suppose I thought Well I should try to get married. And all those years, I just never met anyone that was right for me or…I just didn't find the right person.

And you were active in the pro-life movement all these years?

I was active in the pro-life movement, but once I got into CL, it was more all-encompassing, more total life, not just focused on one particular issue. It was more living the faith in every aspect of life. It was very similar to being in the Missionaries of Charity in a way. It took everything I had. And I really liked that. I've always liked that. I've always wanted to be totally and completely immersed in something. I met tons of people my age.

Wait, I want to back up. Didn't you tell me there was a time... your politics were very right-wing, right?

Oh yes. Extremely right wing for quite a while.

Like when? What years?

Well I think when I met CL that started to change. That's when I started to realize that following Christ is not following a political movement or even a good cause.

When you say right-wing, what do you mean? You were pro-war...

Yeah. I didn't think there was anything wrong with the death penalty, for example.

So you were kind of hard on criminals type of thing.

Yeah, I probably was. I mean it was just an ideology, it wasn't really my heart. My heart was always compassionate. Of course that developed over the years. I mean if someone had come up to me and said, Spare my life, I probably would have done it, but as far...I don't know...I hadn't thought it through very well but if you'd come up to me and asked, "Are you for capital punishment?" I would have said, "Oh yeah"... So there was a split between what I thought and what was in my heart.

But then things started to change. When you're hard core right-wing, you don't care about making friends. You just want to throw the book at everybody, point the finger…I was making friends now and the Italians [the CL movement started in Milan] helped me to change my views. But I was very hard on myself and I was very hard on everyone else. That probably led to my unraveling, too. Because if I couldn't do something well, I just felt terrible. I also had a terrible eating disorder, I was a compulsive overeater for a while. But those things all started to change over the years when I really met the humanity of Christ in such a vibrant way. It wasn't that I hadn't met it in the Missionaries of Charity, but I wasn't in the right place with myself back then. Meeting people, valuing friendships…people wanted to know what I thought as much as what I'd experienced…no-one had ever wanted to know that before…

Okay, and then what happened?

Okay, mid-nineties I started to become interested in consecrated life in CL. They have a group called Memores Domini. And I lived in community with these consecrated women. We worked, I was a teacher, I taught ESL in the city university system.

Tell us what consecrated means. Your virginity, right, your sexuality?

Yeah, I was a novice. I hadn't taken the promises—we don't take vows, we make promises. I'd been there five years and it was approaching the time that I would make my profession.

And the promises would be?

Poverty, chastity, obedience.

Chastity, though, meaning, cause even married people are called to chastity, you're not gonna have sex.

Right.

And you're gonna be single.

Yes.

So you're mulling this over...

No, I was in it. I was living in a Memores Domini house for five years. And I'm preparing to make my profession.

So even though this is a lay movement...is this under the auspices of the Church?

Yeah, it's a consecrated lay community…and it was similar in many ways to how I lived in the Missionaries of Charity. But anyway, I'm living in this group and I was also a member of a theater company called the Blackfriars. And there was a guy in the theater group, his name was David, and we became very good friends. And David worked with the homeless on the George Washington Bridge where he would help people get shelter, get off drugs or alcohol, whatever it was. And he wanted me to meet this guy Frank who he worked with. He said, "Frank is a really nice guy, but he needs friends. He needs real Christian, Catholic friends. He was raised Catholic but he had a troubled past. He was involved with homelessness also and crack." Supposedly he wasn't using crack any more, though that turned out not to be true.

And Frank is black.

Yes. His family's from the Virgin Islands but he was born here so he'd be a black African-American. So I said, "Sure, I'll meet him," so I went to the bridge and Dave was there with Frank and they were both seeing people with problems. And Frank came over and I just said, "Hi, I'm Rita." Frank has a very nice way about him, a good way of communicating.

He's a big guy, right?

He's tall and at that time he was very skinny. He was wearing shoes that were too small. I remember him telling me, "I'm having a hard time walking." I could see he was having a hard time. He was still living in a shelter. And I could see what Dave was saying, that Frank really did need more than what he was getting in the way of friendship at the shelter.

Okay so let's see if…the long and the short of it is that you and Frank are now married with two kids…how old are they?

Six and almost eight….

Okay, so just tell how they came about. You met, you courted…

Again, the same thing that had happened at the Missionaries of Charity began to happen at Memores Domini. I started to have a really hard time. Only this time it was much worse. I was much older; the stakes were a lot higher.

You had a hard time in what sense?

Just crying. Not functioning.

Okay, but why?

Because I think I was in the wrong place, but I didn't have the courage… five years of my life, and I didn't have the courage to ditch the whole thing and say, "This ain't for me."

And why did you feel it wasn't for you?

Because something was missing.

And what did you think was missing?

I think it was a man.

And you knew that.

No. I just knew I was so unhappy.

This is before or after you met Frank?

Before.

Before. Okay. Interesting.

I was starting to...things were starting to get difficult. I think being in the theater, just being out there, exposed to different people and not living...having a little more freedom, I started to have greater longings, let's say...

Were you thinking about children?

I really really tried to suppress that. But what happened was the women in the house and I went on vacation and I ruined the whole time for everybody. These were hard, hard-working women, we all were, and vacation time was really important, to just get a chance to rest. And I was so restless because I said, "This is not my idea of a vacation." And they said, "Well, what is?" And I said, "There should be children around. It's not a vacation if you're just laying on a beach, that just seems very"...I was not comfortable with that. I wanted children around.

So that kind of vacation seemed kind of hedonistic, or just empty?

To me it did. Although to them it was important because they worked hard. I mean these were doctors, teachers, scientists....They were great. They were trying to make me happy but...they just couldn't. After a while I was just so miserable. Finally, Giorgio, who was the Superior from Italy, wrote me an e-mail, because he knew I was suffering. I was seeing a psychiatrist, I was on anti-depressants, and nobody knew how to help me and finally in an email he said, "Rita, just do those things that make you happy. The cross is not your business. That's Jesus's business. You choose the things that make you happy." So I said, "All right." And at this time Frank had gone through all this stuff, and we were in touch with each other...

Now had you been dating?

No. No. We were friends but he was gone. Frank had his own problems. He'd gone back to using crack...actually, he'd never stopped using crack, come to find out. He'd gotten to an all-time low. He wanted to kill himself. He wanted to jump in front of a subway. He wasn't showing up at work, which wasn't like him. So basically he ended up in a shelter, a rehab, and that was the last time he ever used drugs. And then we started writing letters, and we became friendly after that, but it was always me and Frank and Dave. It was always the three of us. Then, after I had my nervous breakdown and I couldn't even work anymore and was staying in a different [Memores Domini] house just to get a break and a change of scenery, and I got this call out of the blue from Frank saying, "Where are you? What's going on?" I really did appreciate that, his reaching out to me and I kind of told him, I didn't want to tell him the whole story, I just said I was having a hard time. But at that time there was no romantic thing going on or anything like that.

Until one day months later I took a wrong turn home from jury duty and I ended up right in front of his job, because at that time he was working as a counselor in aftercare, he'd done very well in this rehab and then he was actually counseling drug addicts. So we just ran into each other accidentally and we just started talking and I think that was the beginning. When things started to get different between us. But up to that time I had never thought of any kind of relationship beyond friendship at all.

It was the wrong turn that was the right turn.

Yes. I was so mad at myself: how could I have taken the wrong bridge home from jury duty? But I remember we talked and afterward we looked at each other and he said, "You made my day. This is the best thing that's happened to me all day." And I thought Wow. Because I felt like such a loser! I was so depressed, I'm thinking I can't even work, thank God I at least had jury duty to go to. And someone said to me, "You just made my day." When I felt like such a loser. I wasn't making anyone's day, I was making everyone miserable. First and foremost, myself. And I thought, Wow. That's what I want. I want to be able to make someone's day. I don't want to be a liability; I want to be a help.

I think that was the beginning of it, when I felt I might be able to be of use to somebody. I felt so terrible about myself. Here I wanted to give my whole life to Christ. I'd always felt that. For as long as I could remember. And I just felt like I'm doing no service to anybody. So when someone said to me, "You just made my day"...I was so moved. And he was so sincere. And I was like, What does he see? What could he possibly see? And so that was the beginning. And I knew after three months probably from that day...I knew that I was in love with him. And it was really terrifying.

Because first of all I knew I had to leave Memores Domini and that was a very difficult thing because I really loved them. The same with the Missionaries of Charity. I don't have anything against them at all. I loved these women. They were like sisters to me. And yet, I had to go. Because I just could not find my happiness there.

So that was scary.

Yes, but Giorgio said to me, "Do what it is that makes you happy," and I thought, "Well, it makes me happy to talk to Frank on the phone. Because I make his day. And he means it. When he talks to me, he's happy. And I'm happy, too."

And then it must have been scary cause there's also this thing of you're white, he's black; you're this girl who was going to be a nun, he's a crackhead, or was. I mean the setup is almost comical.

It was very intense because when I finally left Memores Domini, I thought, "Good, now Frank and I can finally start to date," you know, verify our relationship, he ran away from me! He just changed his tune.

And meanwhile, you've had a huge, totally unexpected turn in your life. A long, long way from thinking you're going to be a nun in the Missionaries of Charity…

He said something very interesting to me that I'll never forget. He said to me, "Rita, for a man like me to be with a woman like you would be like climbing Mt. Everest." And I said to him——[almost whispers] "But nothing is impossible for God." So we both knew that if we didn't have God we wouldn't make it. That was from the beginning. We both knew what was at stake.

You knew you'd need a ton of help.

Yes.

And, if it's okay, you saved yourself for the wedding night?

That, I don't want to...

Okay, the only reason I remotely bring it up, segueing into the marriage thing, is that culturally we're taught that the more people you've slept with, the better, more or less...let me ask you this then. What was your view of the sacrament of marriage going in?

What was my view?

Vis-à-vis...you're Catholic, and we're called as Catholics not to have sex outside of marriage.

Well that was the Mt. Everest of our so-called courtship, the thing that we disagreed about most. That was the reason we broke up three times.

That's a good way to put it.

He'll back that up. We just could not see eye-to-eye. Forget about it. For me, it was hell.

But then you got married, so afterwards it was okay.

No! It was still difficult. Then it became difficult for him. He was like, "Oh, so NOW it's okay for us to be together?" He didn't like these rules and regulations, that authority, that there was some kind of authority over him telling him what he could and couldn't do, the way he saw it. So then it became difficult for him. It was not easy, but I learned a very important thing from that. What it really means to be with somebody in a marriage. And it's work. It's not like everybody says, try it out, see if the you and the person…no, it's a work. It's a journey. It's not something you can establish in a one-night stand.

I mean to be with another person, it takes work. It takes love. It takes sacrifice. And then we had to be open to children! We got married in the Catholic church. Frank didn't expect to have more kids. He's nine years older than me. He already had two grown children. He wasn't ready to raise little kids. That was not in his mind or plan at all. So I said, "Well, we're getting married in the Church, we need to say that we can accept children." We had one child right away. I mean I was already 40 so it was amazing. Then, a year and a half later, we had another child. [Laughing] Frank was like, This is ridiculous.

Two boys, right?

Yes, Micah and Martin.

So Frank was like, This is ridiculous. . .

Yeah, he felt like an old guy having young kids. I didn't even know being 40 if I'd be able to conceive...so it was a blessing. I saw it as a blessing. And then...I mean I come from a family of ten, I didn't want to have just one kid. That's what would have been ridiculous to me, and to have no kids would have been even more ridiculous. I couldn't even imagine....I mean I said to Frank, "We don't even have a lot in common, what are we going to talk about every day? If we don't have kids we're in trouble." [Laughing]. I mean let's be realistic here.

And don't get me wrong. Frank was happy. He loves his kids. We actually practiced natural family planning and that didn't work. It didn't work because we didn't do it right and then we did an even more advanced method called the Creighton model. So here I am 43 years old and I have to try not to conceive and we had to go to these more advanced classes... but this is what I mean, this is part of the whole thing...I mean here's this guy who's lived on the streets for many years. For him, sex, drugs, back then they all went together. And now we're talking about abstaining on certain days...I mean this was just completely foreign to him. So off his radar.

So it's been a stretch for both of you.

Yes. And for the one person to try and understand the other...very difficult. But I think that he gradually started to embrace Catholicism because of CL. He started becoming more involved, going to weekly meetings, started to have people around him, not just me, but families; men, who were living the kind of life that we were trying to live. He saw that it was possible. And that made it much easier. Community made it much, much easier.

But still it's work.

Yes, I mean...the work for me, I don't know what he would say about this, but the work for me was persevering in what I knew was true.

With respect to?...the teachings of the Church, you mean.

Yeah, in that way. Without blaming him for not understanding. And really hanging in there, that's a difficult thing, and also loving.

And how do you find motherhood?

I love being a mother, but it is difficult...

Cause you don't like to cook for one thing.

No, I don't like to cook, as the Missionaries of Charity will attest.

The reason I ask is, marriage is basically ordered to something higher than just the husband and wife. Usually, that's children and therefore a marriage needs to be open to them....of course I've never had kids...but just as this there's this kind of fairy-tale cultural overlay to marriage there's a fairy-tale cultural overlay to motherhood. We supposedly just love our children to death and we cuddle and everything's Instagram-beautiful, 24/7. It seems to me the reality would be that having children is a crucible, just like marriage.

I've met mothers who are a lot less stressed out than me and they have a lot more kids, too... Just amazing.

Right. Some mothers seem to be born to it.

But also I've felt very keenly that the culture we live in does not welcome children. It's a contraceptive mentality that dominates. If you have a child, it's your choice, so you have to deal with all the problems that come with it, in spite of Hilary Clinton's "It takes a village." I also came to motherhood so late. I lived so many years without kids that all of a sudden. So being older, the energy it takes to care for kids, constantly, came as a bit of a shock.

Especially after having a life of your own.

And I also had a lot of religious training. I remember someone asked my friend Jonathan, who's a father, "Jonathan, when do you have time for personal prayer?" Jonathan replied jokingly, "Uh, between three and four in the morning."

So I was used to a life of silence where I prayed and I studied and I wrote my poetry. That was my life and all of sudden I couldn't do that anymore. I mean now that they're older and in school I'm starting to be able to. But when your kid's hungry and wants to eat you can't say...

"Hold on, let me finish this stanza..."

Or read my Office, or whatever it is. So it was an adjustment because I really believed my way of "holiness" was the best way but you have to adjust that and say, No, feeding my child IS praying the Office. Taking care of my husband IS writing my poem. It was a huge adjustment in that sense.

Also I was used to going out to work every day. I mean I don't miss that that much, but...

Just so people know, Frank works and he's...

He's a doorman.

In Manhattan.

Yes.

And he works the night shift.

Yes.

We were talking a couple of weeks ago about your anniversary. He wanted to go out, just the two of you, and...

Don't get me wrong, there's nothing wrong with a husband and wife going out on their own. That's a beautiful thing and I think husbands and wives should do that. I'm not against that at all. I just feel at this particular point in my life...but I guess I've always felt this...it's consistent with the way I've always been. I just want my life to be a total gift. And I want it to be shared with everyone. So when we went out for our anniversary I said, " Let's invite our family and friends. Who are able to be there with us. Because our marriage has a task. And it's not just me and you staring at each other and getting what we can from each other to fulfill our needs. It's something that I desire to live with others." I enjoy the fact that people want to be with my husband, to share their lives with him also. It's not just me. I don't have to possess every minute of his time; he doesn't have to be paying attention every minute to me and the kids.

So that kind of grasping possession that ruins a lot of marriages, that we all hate, especially guys...

Right, has to go. And it's not like I wasn't insecure in the beginning, especially since when we got married, we came from two very different places. Just being married…I'd never been married before, I didn't know what to expect, I didn't even know what emotions were going to come out of me. It was all very new for me.

How old were you when you got married?

39, almost 40. At first, I had moments of insecurity where I'd get jealous if Frank were talking to another woman. But as time rolled on, I saw people really love my husband. And they love him because they see Christ in him. I know how important it is…I desire for the world to meet Christ. And if the world can meet Christ through my husband, and I can facilitate that in some way, that makes me happy. I don't need to possess him all for myself.

At the same time, of course, it's not like you're out cheating on each other. In another way, the boundary is very firm.

I think when…a Christian, Catholic, sacramental marriage, and maybe all marriages in some way, I don't know, but I can speak from my own experience, we are at the service of the Church. Our lives together, I feel very strongly because I wouldn't be happy any other way, our lives together have a task. We have a task as a couple. And that really is to live Christ. To build the kingdom of God. And you can't do that if you are sucking the life blood out of the other person, and if you don't trust the other person. But you don't even think of that after a while. What's important is the task of the relationship.

Plus you have kids. And kids, as we were saying the other day, without kids you can bolt when conflict arises. But kids make it so you kind of have to work it out.

Yeah. There's a lot more at stake. You love these kids and that's part of the task.

When I say task, I mean in a positive sense. We're thrown into the world and we ask, Why the hell am I here? To have a task is a wonderful thing. To have a purpose. We need it. And it's not enough for me to say, "Oh, I have a really nice husband and really cute kids and we're going to buy a house and"...No, that's not what I want. I want my whole family to be building the kingdom of God. I don't know how that's going to happen. I can't predict that...I mean I hope and pray my children will love the Church and have the desire I have and that my husband has. But I don't know that. Nonetheless it's a wonderful thing to be able to give your life for another, for the greater good. I wouldn't be happy any other way, I just wouldn't. To make life about how much I can accumulate for myself and my family would be a real drag. I wouldn't know what the point was. Because my heart, my desire, are so great I just could never live like that.

That's beautiful. You were saying the other day that feminism isn't the way to come into our full womanhood; Christ is.

[Long pause]. Something my husband told me, I don't know if I've told you this, this is something new that he said to me recently. When we were struggling in our courtship if you can call it that, he gave me a really hard time. And he was going through a lot. Getting off drugs, trying to start his new life, and he had had many, many relationships with women. He did not trust women for anything. At all. And when we started dating, I was in a very vulnerable position. Because I was really scared. I thought I would never get married. And I would never have children. And that put me in a very vulnerable position. What the hell was I going to do with my life? I'd been ousted already...no, ousted isn't the word: I'd failed already in two consecrated endeavors...and I really wanted a task, a vocation, like I was saying, a purpose, a direction. And so I was kind of nutty. Because the more he gave me a hard time and pulled away from me, the more crazy I got.

So after you started dating, he kind of disappeared.

Yeah, for a while. And the other day he said, "As crazy as you were, I saw the humanity of Christ in you." He said, "Remember, I did not trust a single woman any more. But as crazy as you were, the humanity of Christ is what led me to trust."

So his heart was really open.

He said, "That's how I encountered Christ. The person of Christ, in the flesh. Through you. So it didn't even matter that you were nutty."

What do you mean when you say nutty, you mean just kind of calling him and stalking him and stuff?

Yeah, like calling him all the time and crying like crazy every time I felt like he was rejecting me. But I was very, very vulnerable. I couldn't bear to be rejected. It was just so painful. This longing was real. I was longing for my vocation because I'd been trying so hard for so many years. I felt like I was finally going to be put where I belonged. And I had to have that answer. I couldn't live without it. And it made me nuts, it made me crazy that I was so close to it and it felt like it was moving away from me. And he couldn't understand that and at the same time he couldn't get rid of me because there was something so true…He told me later that he was saying to himself, "What am I doing with this woman, she's so crazy?" And then he said, "But wait a minute, I'm crazy, too!" He realized we were both extremely weak. And it was only Christ who was going to be able to pull us through. But it required that kind of surrender.

On both your parts.

Yeah. On my part more of a patience, more of a trust. I had to be patient and trust that sooner or later he was gonna marry me. And on his part he had to trust that he was going to marry me. That he wasn't going *to screw it up. Because Christ was going to sustain us. And he told me he's very proud. That's one of the things he's most proud of in life, that he's been married for nine years! And he's got two children. He's providing for them. I mean he is so happy about that! He always tells me that. And every time we have an anniversary he'll say you know, however many years it is, Now we've been married seven, eight, nine years! Joy. It's a victory. He's climbed Mt. Everest!*

Our culture tells us that happiness lies in unbridled freedom, in license. So it's interesting that it instead lies as you say in having a task. Around which everything becomes ordered. And then… "My yoke is easy and my burden light." Even though…it's sacrifice.

Well, I think as Christians we are hard-wired to give of ourselves completely. We can't help it.

As humans!

As humans but I think as Christians ontologically, by virtue of our baptism, a grain of seed… "Unless a seed falls to the ground and dies it remains alone. But if it dies it yields a rich harvest." So I think by virtue of our baptism, that is something we can't help. We long to give of ourselves completely. To die to ourselves so that something new can be born. And for me it's very real, the desire that I have to give of myself, to be a complete gift. You know yesterday when you were talking about Ruth Burrows, was it Ruth Burrows, that Carmelite?

Yes.

You were talking about how she says that when we pray, it's really God taking the initiative. It's really Him. It's not what we do, but what He does. And that really struck me and I was thinking about that and thinking about that. What is that, what is that? And I was thinking when I say to my husband or to anybody, I love you, I mean it. I, I, love you. And yet who is able to say that, really? Only Christ can say that. So then who is "I"?

I live now not I, but Christ lives in me...

Yeah, but it's not like Christ jumps out of us. It's not like he's some energy that's released from us.

It's not like Invasion of the Body Snatchers...

No, he becomes one with our I. I love you and I really love you. Who loves you? It's me, it's Rita. But it's also Christ.

It's fascinating because we don't lose our individuality. We're not all squished into this amorphous faceless mass of humanity. Instead we're actually brought to the height of our uniqueness through disappearing in Christ.

Yeah. He grows in us. He becomes the definition of our "I." I don't think it's right when you say to someone Jesus loves you. No, I love you.

Andwe'renotthesame.RitaisnotHeatherisnotFrankisnotMicahis not Martin.

No, but we're part of the same thing. Because what Frank said, he saw Christ's humanity in me, he saw the love Christ had for him in me. But it's me that loves. And it's Christ that he loves. I mean we are so entwined.

I think that's a really great place to end. "We are so entwined." That's perfect.

Frank Simmonds died of neuroendocrine cancer on January 19, 2015.

❧ JOHNNY, FELICIA, AND SOREN: AN ADOPTION STORY

Johnny Goraj is a singer-songwriter. His wife Felicia is a pediatric nurse.

They met at Children's Hospital in LA where John was working as a trauma tech.

"We somehow saw each other as human beings rather than through a veil of lust or obsession," Johnny says. Felicia continues,

"I saw his spirit and he saw mine. Even though we had a ten-year age gap, I thought, 'This person is full of love and someone I want to be around.' "

Felicia had been raised Protestant. Johnny's a cradle Catholic. Almost from the time they met till the time they got married, they went to Mass together every Sunday.

Felicia: "I was always drawn to working with kids, but marriage and children had never been on my radar. Not until I met Johnny did I trust anyone enough to make that commitment, to enter into the sacrament, to raise a child together."

"That was miraculous to me. That was a conversion."

Felicia told Johnny up front that for certain biological reasons she wasn't sure she could physically bear a child.

"Johnny said, 'No problem! We're just going to trust God.' He didn't waver for a second."

So they got married. Felicia was 37½ by that time; Johnny was 27. Instantly their focus went to getting pregnant. "We trust God but what day is it in my cycle? There was a lot of sadness, and grief, and fear around lack of control. If God creates life, why won't He create it in me? Why am I being set apart?"

In the infertility world, they also discovered, everything becomes medical. Everything was charted, measured. There wasn't a lot of fun, of play. There was fear, stress.

After a year, they realized, "This needs to stop. This is not the way we want to have children."

They suddenly saw that they wanted to be parents way more than they wanted to be pregnant.

A huge burden fell from their shoulders. Their whole focus shifted. They'd just moved to Nashville, for Johnny's music. They found a parish they loved.

John made the initial calls to adoption agencies. "I was done with the sorrow. I was ready."

They completed the home study—a thorough vetting process—through Catholic Social Services.

They were first presented with African-American twins, the product of rape. "John said, 'Absolutely!' We ended up saying no because we weren't comfortable with the ethics of the agency."

Then, through a friend, they found a couple in South Dakota. The husband belongs to a prestigious nation-wide academy of adoption lawyers. Beth, the wife, has a passion for working with young birth mothers in the most difficult situations.

One day Beth called. "There's a potential birth mom in Georgia, but she's high-risk. Extreme poverty. Appalachia. And she's already had a disruption with her first pregnancy"—meaning she'd planned to give the baby up for adoption, then changed her mind mid-stream.

Johnny and Felicia decided to move forward anyway. They drove to the Smoky Mountains in winter. They met Mandy and her mother at a MacDonald's.

"It was terrifying. We were shaking. We'd prayed beforehand:

Help us bring love, help us bring love."

Desperate to make conversation, Felicia blurted, "So—do you guys hike? Do you do yoga?"

"They just stared at me. They were like, 'Can you buy us some food?' They were bringing home a roadkill deer."

Mandy was 7½ months pregnant.

"A twenty-year-old with no teeth, of course you think of meth. It didn't seem like that but we didn't know the world she lived in. We weren't sure she even had a house."

With all that, the two fell in love with her and Mandy "kind of fell in love with us." Felicia had started RCIA in Nashville. She and Johnny decided to go forward. We have to think of the child, they kept telling themselves.

Mandy asked Felicia to be with her during the C-section. Both she and Johnny were at the hospital when Soren was born.

"There's a lot of joy and a lot of sadness. You're getting a child and someone else is losing a child. Still, I still think Mandy knew in her heart of hearts: 'I have to do this.'"

Mandy had ten days after the birth to change her mind. Felicia and Johnny were terrified the whole time that she would.

Soren turned out to be in withdrawal. The doctors were never sure why. It wasn't necessarily because Mandy was on drugs. The baby had to be put on methadone and go into the NICU for three weeks. Johnny and Felicia stayed on and visited him every day.

Last fall, the family returned to LA. The adoption is open. Their relationship with Mandy continues.

As we wind up our conversation, Soren is eating a banana and crooning.

"We go in and check on him fifty times a night," says Johnny. "We send each other pictures of him constantly. We rejoice at this beautiful son we're being allowed to care for."

Felicia adds, "Sometimes we look at each other and say, 'Thank God we went through all this pain.'"

"Thank God we never decided to walk away."

Their eyes meet across Soren's high chair.

"Thank God we couldn't get pregnant."

THE HOMILY I'D GIVE IF I WERE A PRIEST

Now don't get me wrong: I love priests. I have no desire to be a priest. Priests are doing just fine.

Still, personally I would like to hear more homilies on the beauty of the Narrow Gate! On the fact that Christ calls us to come fully awake, fully alive, fully open to joy. On the truth that joy doesn't come from following a rule book, constantly peering around to make sure everyone else is following the rule book, or cultural lemminghood. Of course when we're awake in love, we're not going to cheat on our spouse. Of course we're not frittering away our life energy on judging, hating, and excluding.

Of course we are going to feel our own pain and loneliness and hunger and fear very deeply, so deeply that at times it seems it cannot be borne. We're going to be pruned into compassion. That is our whole value as followers of Christ: we allow our suffering to make us available and vulnerable to the suffering of the world; to the terrible sexual and emotional wound at the heart of mankind.

To that end, here's the homily I'd give if I were Priest For a Day:

"To be a follower of Christ is to participate in the victory of love over fear. And just on the off-chance we've veered from our place at the back of the church with the tax collector, folks [see Luke 18:9-14] , we're not "following the rules" so we can look good in the eyes of our also-following-the-rules fellow church-goers. Come my brothers and sisters! Those people were the PHARISEES! Those were the people who killed, and who continue to kill, Christ! Catholicism is not a country club whose members we vet to ensure we're in the "right" company! The very thought should turn our stomachs!

Here's how we know our lives in Christ are bearing fruit:

In spite of our own suffering, loneliness, and pain, we're welcoming. We're warm. We're kind (or we're at least shooting for those things, and not just toward the people who can "do" something for us, but everyone). We're in immediate, intimate contact with a few active drunks; someone who's headed into or has just emerged from a psych ward; an incarcerated felon or two; several women who have had abortions and are in silent, excruciating mourning; at least one stripper; several people in desperately unhappy marriages, about to be evicted from their apartments, or dying; a minimum-wage worker or two; at least three people who are certifiably insane; at least one U.S. Army chaplain and one peace activist (even better if they're both priests and the latter is in solitary confinement in a federal prison); several homeless people; and a whole TON of gay people, transgender folks, and sex and love addicts of all stripes.

If that's not part of your circle—in my case, that *is* my circle—you're not getting out enough. If you aren't sharing your struggles and heart with that circle, at the very least in prayer, something is wrong. Because those are the people Christ hung out with. Because "those people" are us: the people. The only people. Suffering, struggling humans. Because if we're going to be inviting people to a life of poverty, chastity and obedience, we sure as hell better be inviting each other into our homes, our tables, our hemorrhaging, conflicted hearts.

If we're afraid all that is going to "lower our standards," we're very much mistaken. There's no lower standard than self-righteous fear.

Share the joy, man. Tell a joke. Lighten up. Eat a meal with some friends. Exchange stories of how we're walking toward the light. One morning we'll wake up and realize that we are "following the rules" and then some. We're not going to Mass just on Sundays, but every other day—because there's nowhere else we'd rather be. We're not going to just three recovery meetings a week, but five—plus a trip to the jail to talk to the drunks there. We'll realize that though we haven't added it up, we're probably giving away at least ten percent of our money.

We'll realize: I actually let that guy who cut me off in traffic yesterday off the hook. I actually felt a stab of what felt suspiciously like affection toward my mother-in-law, my junkie son, my sex-worker neighbor, the Marine Corps soldier, the bleeding-heart liberal (depending on your stance, one of these is sure to be difficult), my boss (bonus points if you're self-employed), the young girl who, from a one-night-stand with a guy whose last name she never caught, is having a baby.

We'll realize: Oh. THIS is what Christ meant! I don't have to be boiled in oil or have my eyes gouged out. This is laying down my life: this sharing, this exchange, this richness, this mercy, this mystery.

We'll realize that love is a way more tender—and way more exacting Master—than fear."

#ALLOFUS

When we fail to follow the teachings of Christ, the first to suffer, to bear the brunt of the untruths, are children.

Children and women.

I'm not talking about we privileged, well-educated women who have been the recipients of every right known to humankind and who in many cases are still unsatisfied, who are petulant, who want yet more.

I'm talking about the "simple," "provincial" women the world over: the poor who, as usual, are going about their business of toil, suffering, mothering and love. I'm talking about the women who are wiser than many of us and who are saving us.

What must such a woman think upon hearing a Hollywood movie starlet rant about the "trauma" of auditioning for a part in an NC-17 movie with a powerful mogul and who is shocked—shocked!— when he suggests having sex? Who thirty years ago suffered the "indignity" of having a man place his hand on her back to usher her into a room? Who at a posh cocktail party—the horror!—was once propositioned.

That's not trauma. Trauma is to have your husband "disappeared" by the secret police. Trauma is to live in a war zone, or to be held, often indefinitely in an immigrant detention camp, or as a refugee. Trauma is not having enough money to feed your kid, or educate your kid, or take your kid to the doctor.

My friend Tensie and her husband Dennis work with Latino farm workers, many of them undocumented, on California's central coast. They distribute clothing and food. They both run interference with doctors, hospitals, and Social Security. Tensie holds a free medical clinic every Thursday.

One of the women she's walked with over the years I'll call Sylvia. One day Tensie told me her backstory.

At the age of thirteen, Sylvia was hanging around her family home minding her own business when a carload of men drove up, grabbed her from the yard, threw her into the back seat and hauled her off to a church to be married to a guy who was thirty years her senior and a drunk.

The guy was kind of a jerk but in her way Sylvie grew to care for him. She had three kids, two boys and a girl. She began working in the strawberry fields, universally acknowledged as some of the hardest manual labor on earth.

Amazingly, however, anger was not Sylvia's primary emotion. The day before, she'd told Tensie, the weather had been so hot in the fields that the foreman had allowed the workers 15 extra minutes in the shade after lunch. "That felt so good, mija!" she'd told Tensie. "I was so grateful."

Mainly she was grateful because those extra fifteen minutes left her that much fresher, after the long workday was finally through, to rush home and prepare the molé for the sixteenth birthday party she and the family were throwing for her daughter that night.

"All she could think of was her daughter," Tensie reported. "She was just beaming, she loves her so much. After another day of back-breaking labor, she couldn't wait to pitch in and do more work, to make the night beautiful—for her daughter."

We fell silent for a moment.

"By the cultural standard," Tensie continued, "she has nothing. But she doesn't have time to feel sorry for herself. She's too busy caring for other people. And it's not because she's stupid. She feels what happened to her keenly. She fully knows that farm workers are over-worked and underpaid. She suffers on account of her husband. But the nobility of spirit...it is really something to behold."

After we hung up, I thought: That is Mary. Giving birth in a stable. Standing steadfast at the foot of the Cross. Head bent in infinite tenderness over her drunk husband, her neighbor's addict son—which is to say over the body of Christ—hand laid with infinite tenderness over his wounded breast.

That is the picture of what woman was born for. To minister to, to comfort, to console, to hold what purports to be stronger.

To support one another, and to help heal the wound between women and men that began in the Garden of Eden.

There's suffering, huge suffering, but there's suffering either way. To be open to new life every time you sleep with your husband, to hold the tension, to long for the male gaze that no woman ever gets quite as fully or in the quite the way she longs for on this earth—to bow before, give birth to, weep anyway—that is Our Blessed Mother. That is the glory of our womanhood.

You cannot serve both God and mammon.

You can't hate men and also purport to love women.

Let me not put my boot on the neck of mankind. Let me instead hold all humankind, broken and bleeding, to my breast.

Instead of #MeToo, let's have #AllOfUs.

❧ | V ❧

RADICAL FREEDOM, RADICAL EXILE

"In order to be free you simply have to be so, without asking permission of anybody. You have to have your own hypothesis about what you are called to do, and follow it, not giving in to circumstances or complying with them. But that sort of freedom demands powerful inner resources, a high degree of self-awareness, a consciousness of your responsibility to yourself and therefore to other people."

—ANDREI TARKOVSKY, *SCULPTING IN TIME*

❧ SAINTHOOD: TO WILL THE ONE THING

The Danish theologian Søren Kierkegaard observed that the saint is the person who wills the "one thing." I wonder if in trying to do many things, we run the risk of failing to bear fruit in any of them.

To that end, I want to mention some of the women who form what I call my personal Communion of Saints. Like me, all of these women were single and celibate. All of these women devoted themselves heart, mind, and soul to Christ.

By any objective measure I don't think any of them would be called shrinking violets.

There's Dorothy Day (1897-1980), co-founder of the lay Catholic Worker movement. Day gave up the love of her life, Forster Batterham, a resolute atheist who objected to having the daughter they'd conceived together baptized. For decades she served the street poor of NYC's Lower East Side. She was one of the most important thinkers and writers of the 20th century. She subscribed to old-school Catholic practices: retreats, the Office, daily Mass.

She lived in voluntary poverty, entitled her autobiography *The Long Loneliness*, and frequently went to jail for acts of civil disobedience. She also observed, "The greatest challenge of the day is: how to bring about a revolution of the heart, a revolution which has to start with each one of us."

Mother Teresa, now canonized, needs no introduction. She served the dying lepers and untouchables of Calcutta, founded the Missionaries of Charity, and is known world-wide as the face of Christ. Along the way, she experienced a 50-year dark night of the soul. Fifty years. That is one fierce woman. After decades of prayer, work, and "joyful participation in the sorrows of the world," she could say: "We can do no great things; only small things, with great love."

Flannery O'Connor (1925-1964), one of the greatest writers the Church—hell, the world—has ever produced, lived with her mother on a dairy farm in Milledgeville, Georgia, suffered all her adult life, without a word of self-pity, from the lupus that would kill her, and died at 39.

Her novels (*Wise Blood* and *The Violent Bear It Away*), award-winning short stories, collected letters (*The Habit of Being*), and essays (*Mystery and Manners: Occasional Prose*) sustain, console and challenge. Almost everything she wrote is quotable. Among my favorites: "The Catholic writer, in so far as he has the mind of the Church, will feel life from the standpoint of the central Christian mystery: that it has, for all its horror, been found by God to be worth dying for."

Caryll Houselander (1901-1954), was a British mystic, poet and spiritual writer who had a special heart for traumatized children, wore a pair of big round tortoiseshell glasses, lived in London during the Blitz, and until she died at 53 from breast cancer, apparently barely slept or ate.

She suffered an unrequited love for a British spy—by all accounts a wastrel—who was the model for Ian Fleming's "James Bond." She had an eclectic coterie of friends and was utterly devoted to Christ.

Houselander was not perfect. She swore, drank and smoked. She had a sharp tongue. And she was a wonderful storyteller. She once wrote:

I was running someone down [to a priest], saying beastly things
of him. Suddenly I noticed that [the priest's] eyes were shut. "You
are not listening," I said. He replied, "I cannot—not to that; you
see we are both present at the Mass. Whilst you were trying to
make me think ill of X, Christ our Lord was offering Himself up
to God to redeem him."

"But we are not at Mass," I said...and he said, "When your
thoughts are hard or bitter or sad, let the sanctuary bell silence
them. Somewhere, it is always ringing."*

In a 1954 review of the book *Caryll Houselander and the Flowering*
of Christ, Dr. Janet Golden observed:

[Houselander] is that rarity among Catholic writers, a woman
who has produced a substantial body of serious work...the
difficulty is to find those women, with the exception of the
novelists, who have written more than two or three books; for whom
writing is a career rather than the by-product of a life which has
centered itself somewhere else...
[P]erhaps the simplest [explanation for this state of affairs] is
that a woman's creativeness tends to disperse itself: in children,
in making a home, in personal relationships. Not many women
have the ambition or the single-minded tenacity that is needed
to sustain a career of writing. They simply do not have enough of

themselves left over to put down on paper, day after day, week after week, year after year…

In a world in which masculine values are so dominant, there is a real need for women who will write as women——not blue-stockings, or female Ernest Hemingways, but women who delight in being what they are. Father Gerald Vann underlines this need in his latest book, "The Water and the Fire":

> *'Of all the trends we have been considering as characteristic of the world today——the increasing loss of wisdom and vision, of stillness, of Nature, of the stability of home and family life, of symbol——it seems true to say that they represent something particularly alien to the nature of woman.…Our troubles spring from the overemphasis on the masculine in our world,' and he adds, 'precisely because the nature of the psychological crisis through which we are passing is what it is, woman has an unique opportunity to redeem the situation.'* *

I'm not good for much else, but I do seem to have been graced with "the ambition or the single-minded tenacity that is needed to sustain a career of writing." Such women have no mentor, helpmeet, cheerleader, companion, or assistant. We have no-one in our daily lives who says "Good work," or "That was brave" or "You were kind to meet with that out-of-town reader even though you were exhausted and wanted to go grocery shopping and get your hair cut."

That's all just as it should be. Is a mother recognized? Is a wife recognized?

Narrow is the gate.

For those of us women whose vocation is writing, let's not be afraid to enter it.

Let's not be afraid of the exile the narrow gate entails.

THE SPIRITUALITY OF IMPERFECTION: THE SECOND CONVERSION OF ST. THÉRÈSE OF LISIEUX

For weeks now, at the suggestion of my spiritual director, I've been carrying around a yellow Post-It in my wallet. On it are written the following directives:

— *I'm not responsible for making people happy or always doing what they need.*
— *I need to have a life first before I'm equipped to help others.*
— *I'm responsible for seeing to it that my needs are met.*

I cannot begin to describe how thoroughly, how painfully, each of those grate against my very identity. I was raised to believe that to be good is always to put the other person first, that love consists in ignoring your own needs, that your job is to make the other person happy.

This may come as news to many of those who are closest to me.

Because what happens, and figuring this out has taken most of my adult life, is that when you try in the wrong way and for the wrong reasons to make other people happy, far from being grateful to you, those people end up either rebelling, or trying to control you, or both. You end up resenting their rebellion. And the whole thing—your sacrifice, your martyrdom—blows up in your face.

Also, if you try in the wrong way and for the wrong reasons to make other people happy, you tend to think, often rightfully, that people are taking advantage of you, because it is human nature to take advantage of someone who has, however inadvertently, placed him- or herself in a position to be hurt.

Which tends to make me, for one, come out fighting. The other person thinks everything's going along fine and suddenly they show up at quarter to five instead of four-thirty and I'm ready to call 9-1-1. "What's the matter?" they innocently ask. "YOU. WERE. LATE!!!" I shriek. I'm not proud of it, but I am bound to report I have actually done that a few times in my life.

I have certainly made progress, and done massive amounts of work in this area, but I'm ever called upon to make more.

Which brings me to one of the most interesting and useful books I've read in a long time: *Everything is Grace: The Life and Way of St. Thérèse of Lisieux*, by Joseph F. Schmidt, FSC, a lecturer, spiritual director, and counselor at the International Renewal Center of the Christian Brothers located in the Sangre de Cristo Mountains near Santa Fe.

A little background: Thérèse (1873-1897) was born into a bourgeois, deeply pious French family, the youngest of five daughters, all of whom would eventually enter the convent. Sickly as an infant, she had to be farmed out to a wet nurse from whom she was later separated. Her mother died of breast cancer when Thérèse was 4 ½. Two of her beloved older sisters, surrogate mothers, left fairly soon after for the cloistered convent at Carmel.

In other words, she had major abandonment issues.

Thérèse herself entered the same convent at the age of fifteen, lived a hidden, outwardly unremarkable life there, and died of TB at the tender age of 24.

She might have remained entirely unknown had she not left behind her autobiography, written under orders. Collated and edited by the sisters into a book, *The Story of a Soul* became an instant bestseller. Thérèse was canonized as a saint a mere 28 years after her death. In 1997, she was named a Doctor of the Church (one of only four women upon whom the honor has been bestowed). Her "little way" continues to inspire, invite, and confound. And people, including me, continue to write books about her.

One of Schmidt's central theses is that Thérèse's path to holiness was grounded largely in her struggle with, to put it in contemporary terms, "co-dependence." Though a pampered, well-disciplined, and treasured child, she was overly-sensitive and touchy. She tended to over-bond and over-emote.

In *Everything is Grace*, he describes the famous Christmas eve during which Thérèse's "second conversion" took place, and she left behind, never to return to, the wrong kind of people-pleasing.

The custom at the time was for the children of the house to leave their empty shoes by the fire for the parents to fill with candy. Thérèse, at 13 the youngest of the five Martin daughters, was the last of the family to keep up this charming ritual. Upon returning from Mass that night, her usually kind father, uncharacteristically cranky, passed the shoes and remarked, "Well, thank heaven, this will be the last year." Thérèse overheard him.

Ordinarily she would have burst into tears and made a scene, devastated at having displeased her dear Papa. She began running upstairs to her room, choking back sobs. But on the moment, something changed.

Schmidt writes:

Originally, in conformity with the family pattern, she had felt that if she did displease her father, she would not survive as the person she was. Her feelings had made her believe that failing to please her father would mean that she was not the good person on which she had staked her identity. Who would she be if she were not the sensitive, pleasing little Thérèse? She felt that she would surely die; it was as simple as that. Her feelings told her that she would

simply no longer exist; that she would dissolve, as it were,
into nothingness. *

But she did not die. She gathered herself, allowed herself to experience but not to be overwhelmed by her feelings of failure and hurt, and marched downstairs like an adult to open her presents with gratitude, good cheer, and joy.

Schmidt continues:

Thérèse was pleasing her father, but not because she needed to
please him in order to make herself feel connected and good. She
was pleasing him now because, from the depths of her true self
with a deepened sense of inner freedom, she could act in whatever
compassionate, creative, and free way she was called to...
[F]rom the time of her complete conversion she would never
walk on the path of accommodating others at the expense of her
own true self...Now she would accommodate others in a spirit
of freedom and creativity, and as an expression of real love. In
pleasing others, she would never again act in violence to her
own integrity. *

Thérèse never afterward had to insist on her own way because in a sense she always got her own way, which was to love, and to be loved by, God in total freedom.

On pilgrimage to Rome the next year, she had occasion to meet and move among many priests. "[I]f their sublime dignity raises them above the angels," as she diplomatically put it, "they are nonetheless weak and fragile men."*

Her solution was not to browbeat, lord it over, criticize, or carp. Her solution was *to pray for priests continuously for the rest of her life.* She who herself wanted to be a priest, a martyr, a saint, knew that the path was to help out, to appeal to God on behalf of all her brothers and all her sisters, to minister to the women with whom she was surrounded in the convent, to the two seminarians to whom she wrote, and by extension to all the world.

A line in one of the Eucharistic prayers at Mass runs, "We thank you for counting us worthy to stand in your presence and minister to you." We're all called to minister, to be bridges, to act in a priestly capacity. If we want to be priests, look around. Are there not zillions of people out there suffering?

Let's not wait for a man (or a woman, for that matter) to validate, instruct or give permission.

Let's go help people out!

 THE BANQUET TABLE

*"There is great satisfaction in remaining faithful; perhaps it is the greatest satisfaction of all. Even if not one knows about your faithfulness, even if no one values it."**

—ALEKSANDR SOLZHENITSYN, *CANCER WARD*

One recent morning at Mass, the priest asked in his homily, "You know what we need more of in the Church?"

Fervent laypeople? I thought. Single people who faithfully, with burning hearts, trudge to Mass? Contemplative hermits in the city? Sober alcoholics to spread the word to all the drunks, including the many priests, in church?

"We need more good Catholic families!" Father exclaimed.

I stifled a snicker: my hopes for being special, singled out, recognized, dashed again. Plus, we do need more good—by which I took the priest to mean ardent, excited, questing—Catholic families.

I have always seen the teachings of the Church on sex as an invitation to sit at the table with the rest of the human family. Otherwise, as a single, husbandless, childless woman past child-bearing age, I would have no place at the table. There is no status lower in our society—unless it's an aging, single, gay man.

Trust me, if that is your status, you feel it. You wash your face and comb your hair and put on a clean shirt, because Christ said don't make a big deal of your fasting, but you feel it: out of and in the Church. You feel it in the unbelievable lack of gallantry, of courtesy, from some—not all by any means, but some—men. You feel it from the cruelty and utter lack of fellow feeling from some—not all by any means, but some—other women.

I feel it and boo-hoo: we all have some huge cross we feel all the time. And the longer I am in the Church, the more I see that without her teachings on sex, and everything else, I would have no place at the table and my life would have no meaning. Because to be in the Church is to be part of the Mystical Body. It's to be in solidarity with everyone, including all those who for whatever reason could not have sex; could not attract, or be, a spouse; could not or were not moved to raise a family. It's to be in solidarity with the old, the unattractive, the disabled, the poor; the misfits and malcontents and die-hard solitaries; the temperamentally unsuited and vocationally unavailable; the sexually, emotionally and physically damaged, wounded, and disordered. Because we are all disordered, in our ways, and we are all responsible for what we do as adults, and we all fail in our duty to the children of the world.

The Church has always had a place for me; it's the secular, youth-oriented, politically correct, rights-based culture to which I would otherwise naturally be drawn (I find the right even less congenial) in which I've never felt at home and that, as I age, has even less of a place for me.

So I didn't take the least offense at Father's remark. I didn't think he was discriminating me, or belittling me, or minimizing my contribution to the Church and to the world. I thought he was saying, in so many words, Isn't it grand that, no matter our station in life, no matter if we're on our deathbeds, we get to offer ourselves up for all of creation? I thought of my three unborn children and of how Catholic tradition has it that we share the same guardian angel. I thought of my six godchildren. I thought about all the young people in my life: the seminarians, the teachers, the writers, the sober drunks and addicts, the whole crazy pageant of people—young and old—with whom I've been blessed; the people who keep me alive and vital and juiced.

Every so often, as I've said, I hear from a woman who asks, "How can you belong to a Church that doesn't allow women to be priests?"

My answer, again, is Man, if you want to be priest, go for it! No-one's stopping you. To be a priest is to be constantly scourged, constantly to stagger under a heavy cross, constantly to comfort others with no-one but the Good Shepherd to comfort you.

To be a priest is to undergo a constant and ongoing death.

It is to know that your time is not your own, your body is not your own, your life is not your own.

In fact, this is precisely the invitation Christ extends to all of us.

True power, if power's what you're after, has nothing to do with being seen, recognized, validated, or awarded. True power has nothing in it of settling a score, setting the other straight, or crowingly grabbing first place.

True power arises from utter and complete surrender to a Power greater than ourselves.

Christ has already given the command to go out and spread the Gospel to the whole world. Go for it. The world is teeming with those in need of pastoral care. You probably live with some of them.

"The harvest is abundant, but the laborers are few," as Christ observed [Luke 10:2]. And as St. Thérèse learned all too well in her short 24 years: "There are no raptures, no ecstasies—only service."

THE GOOD FATHERS

That many priests respond to my work is one of the joys of my life. When my publisher started asking me for blurbs for my third book, *Shirt of Flame* (2011), I immediately thought: *Oh man, I hate this part. I don't know any famous writers. I don't know anyone who's all that crazy about my work.* And suddenly I realized: *My priest friends! I'll ask the priests.*

So I asked Fathers Ron Rolheiser and Lorenzo Albacete and

Peter Cameron and Vincent Nagle and Robert Barron and James Stephen Behrens and they all patiently read my book and gave me beautiful blurbs. Afterward I realized that almost every one of these incredibly overworked men—and this is just from what very little I know of their personal lives—while they were being of service to me had also been engaged in some dire administrative, physical, emotional, and/or spiritual struggle. These men who had absolutely nothing to gain from me had put aside their own suffering, denied themselves leisure, and read and endorsed my book.

Even if priests hadn't liked what I wrote, they would still be treasures. I can hardly think of a more thankless job, a lonelier job, a job with more meager results and more built-in suffering. And I definitely can't think of a group of men—of people—who have been more courteous to me, more solicitous, more appropriate, more kind.

Good priests show us how to serve even as we suffer. If we admire, respect, and love them, we get to do as they do. Your heart was moved by some wonderful priest: okay, beautiful. Pray for him, and for his brothers. Don't develop an unhealthy attachment to him, or try to get him to pay special attention to you or thank you or recognize you. He's busy enough. Go out to the world and do your own kind of good, whatever way is given to you. We will all meet in heaven.

As the novelist François Mauriac observed:

People say that there is a scarcity of priests. In truth, what an adorable mystery it is that there still are priests. They no longer have any human advantage. Celibacy, solitude, hatred very often, derision and, above all the indifference of a world in which there seems to be no longer room for them—such is the portion they have chosen. They have no apparent power; their task sometimes seems to be centered about material things, identifying them, in the eyes of the masses, with the staffs of town halls and of funeral parlors. A pagan atmosphere prevails all around them. The people would laugh at their virtue if they believed in it, but they do not. They are spied upon. A thousand voices accuse those who fall. As for the others, the great number, no one is surprised to see them toiling without any sort of recognition, without appreciable salary, bending over the bodies of the dying, or ambling about the parish schoolyards.[*]

Or as Flannery O'Connor noted in a letter dated December 9, 1958:

It is easy for any child to pick out the faults of the sermon on his way home from Church every Sunday. It is impossible for him to find out the hidden love that makes a man, in spite of his intellectual limitations, his neuroticism, his own lack of strength, give up his life to the service of God's people, however bumblingly he may go about it.[*]

Long may the Good Fathers live.

COME BACK TO THE CHURCH, COME BACK!

Not long ago I read an essay by a lapsed Catholic, so disgruntled that he'd actually left the Church. No mere Pope Francis would induce this guy to re-join. In so many words, he railed against the namby-pamby "'God is love" message he kept hearing. This guy was a cut above the rest of us lightweights. This guy wanted a challenge. This guy wanted to hear about sacrifice. He approvingly quoted Flannery O'Connor: "They think faith is a big electric blanket, when of course it is the cross."

This guy so did not get what Flannery, with her huge sense of humor, and profound love of Christ, got from Day One: the Church *is* the Cross. If you want to be challenged (and ridiculed, and marginalized, and scorned), do major penance and sacrifice, and die to every idea you've ever had about who you are, who God is, and what religion is, become a member of the Catholic church.

And don't expect a medal for it: "When you finally discover that you are just one of the little people, don't conclude that this makes you special," observed French eccentric/lay comic-mystic/lover of the poor Madeleine Delbrêl.

The idea isn't to demand that the Church make herself worthy of us. The idea is to realize that in spite of our unworthiness, we—miracle upon grace upon wonder upon mystery—have been deemed worthy of the Church. "Lord, I am not worthy that you should enter under my roof, but only say the word and my soul shall be healed," we pray, just before receiving the Eucharist. The Eucharist! The Body and Blood of the Savior of the World. I mean this joker thinks the Church that Christ established upon the Rock of Peter is not worthy of *him*?

Here's the Cross of the Church: The Church is not just for me, you, us. It's for everybody. Thus, we don't get to have homilies tailor-made for us, although in another way a homily is always tailor-made, usually in the last way we would have chosen.

The priest has to meet the tentative searcher; the elderly man who has tottered in, aching in every bone in his body, to give thanks; the pregnant teenager; the wife of the CEO whose son is a crackhead dying out on the streets; the crackhead; the guy who's cheating on his wife; the wife; the vet suffering from PTSD; the general who's ordered the killing; the nurse trying to figure out whether to quit her job because her hospital is performing abortions; the woman who's had, or is contemplating having, an abortion.

He has to meet the one who thinks the Church is too hard and the one who thinks the Church is too soft, the one who is rejoicing and the one who is mourning, the one who is mad at God and the one who is falling madly in love with God. He has to meet the eight-year-old and the eighty-year-old. He also has to meet the blowhard, the Pharisee, the one who thinks only *she* is up to being challenged, only she suffers, only she gets it and for God's sake can't we get some decent music.

All in six minutes.

The priest has to do that while performing baptisms, weddings, funerals; while overseeing the fundraising fall festival; while settling parish conflicts; while blessing homes, cars, and candles. He has to do this, day after day, often many times a day, while exhausted, understaffed, impatient, critical and doubtful (i.e. human) himself. He doesn't get to have it his way, all the time, any more than any of us do.

It is one of the glories and gifts of the Church that we don't encourage priests who are "personalities." We don't encourage flamboyance. We encourage humility, plodding perseverance, and service. So perhaps the priest can be forgiven for resorting to saying that God is love, not least of all because God *is* love—just not the love, hardly ever, that we think. Actually, in twenty-two years in the Church, I have never once heard a priest say that "God is love." I've heard priests say our job is to serve the poor, to examine our faults, to forgive our families and friends, to be kind to our neighbor. I've heard a steady stream of Gospel-based homilies that, if not individually wildly compelling, have consistently, slowly, quietly, inexorably led me closer to Christ.

In twenty-two years, I can also count on one hand the number of times a priest, while celebrating Mass, has appeared surly, bored, condescending, or irreverent. This quiet, faithful carrying out of the duties of the office, no matter how disordered the priest may be personally, has set me free to ponder the great mystery and sacrifice of the Mass, to penetrate beneath the surface, to realize that, as Flannery O'Connor observed, the Mass could be celebrated out of a suitcase in a furnace room and it would still be the Mass: the most shocking, scandalous, cataclysmic, glorious, horrifying, sublime act the world ever has or ever could know.

So let me bring my burning heart. Let me make up for what is lacking in the suffering of Christ. Instead of sitting around complaining and carping about the ways the Church "fails" me, maybe I could think about what I could contribute to her.

People erroneously think the Church is confining, but the Church gives us the framework of prayer, the Gospels, the Catechism, the Mystical Body, and the Sacraments—and then we discover to our surprise that we are more or less on our own. The Church trusts that—given our intelligence, good will, and humble, contrite hearts—we will be able to connect the dots.

And the dots are these: We don't get to have someone hold our hand and guide us along the perilous, excruciatingly lonely path to Christ. We don't get to have someone applaud or even notice our hidden life of sacrifice and penance. We don't get to be understood, validated, and comforted every other minute. Instead, while we're being nailed to our own Cross, we get to do those things for someone else.

We'll find that if we truly want to be challenged, we will regard the abysmal ways we've fallen short in this vale of tears, and we will ponder the Sacraments, we will contemplate the teachings of the Gospels, we will reflect till our last breath on the mystery of the Real Body and the Real Blood, and we will realize, in fear and trembling and dawning, crazy praise: *This is the last thing I would have wanted and it is the only thing I have ever wanted.*

For my own part, I've come to realize that only the Church could have pruned, in the gentlest possible way, my craving for attention, impatience, constant criticism, and hyper-judgment, and that simultaneously, while ceaselessly calling me higher, could have assuaged my guilt, bound up my narcissistic wounds, and invited us me to overcome my seemingly bottomless cowardice and fear.

Above all, the Church is the only place that could fulfill my heart that, in spite of my myriad faults, overflows with love.

If we cultivate the eyes to see and the ears to hear, we will discover that the Church is both the lightest yoke and the heaviest cross imaginable. We will begin to understand the meaning of the Sermon on the Mount. We will see that the biggest electric blanket of all is the desire for spiritual excellence: to be seen as having a degree from a kind of divine Ivy League college; to be working out at a kind of religious high-end gym with a mover-and-shaker personal trainer; for others to view our journey to God as interesting, as special, as just a bit of a cut above the ordinary.

The follower of Christ doesn't strive. The follower of Christ surrenders. Not to mediocrity, but to love—and if ever for one second we presume to think that the love of Christ isn't sufficiently "challenging," we have only to look above the altar: to our Redeemer, our Lord and our Savior: lacerated, bleeding, alone.

That is the love the priest is pointing to when he says "God is love." That is the death Christ was facing when, over the Last Supper, he told the disciples, "Love one another as I have loved you." That is the love upon which Flannery O'Connor's heart, mind, intellect and soul were focused, as she suffered from lupus, was conscripted into life-long celibacy, wrote for a public that mostly didn't understand her, watched her beauty, ability to walk, and life ebb away, and died at the tragically young age of 39, all without a single public word of complaint, anger, or self-pity.

If we want to repent of our sins, if we want to do penance, have at it. The Catholic church is certainly not going to stop us. But here's the thing we will learn as we undergo our own Passion: the theater of Catholicism is the Mass, not us. We're not the star; Christ is. "He must increase, but I must decrease" [John 3:30]. "For whoever wishes to save his life will lose it, but whoever loses his life for my sake will find it" [Matthew 16:25]. "Thus, the last will be first, and the first will be last" [Matthew 20:16]. "But when you pray, go to your inner room, close the door, and pray to your Father in secret. And your Father who sees in secret will repay you" [Matthew 6:6].

Christ isn't kidding. Those are not metaphors. It is just in casting our lot with other extremely unpromising, lackluster, humdrum people that we come to see how terribly unpromising, lackluster and humdrum we are ourselves. It is just in the putting up with the thousand day-to-day petty annoyances, in and out of the Church, that sanctity consists. It's just in accepting that things are never the way we want them, that we will not get the spiritual validation or guidance or friends or adulation we long for, that we start to be saints.

It is in offering ourselves up for God to do with what He wills (as opposed to what we think will make us look good) that, with multiple psycho-spiritual crises and usually over a long, long period of time—again, if my own experience is any indication—we are transformed.

This is a nada, an emptiness, a *via negativa* that is not for the faint of heart. Ask St. John of the Cross. Ask Maximilian Kolbe. Ask Dorothy Day. Ask Franz Jägerstätter.

It's worth reflecting that "outsiders" weren't the ones who called for Christ's crucifixion. He was tortured to death by the members of his own religion: his neighbors, his fellow villagers, his former friends. As a sober drunk, I often reflect upon the way that, nailed in agony to the Cross, Christ refused the sour wine mingled with myrrh, the crude narcotic offered by his executioners.

To the last drop, he suffered without anesthesia.

To the last drop of blood, he suffered us.

❧ MY MESSAGE FROM GOD: DRESS APPROPRIATELY FOR MASS

One recent September, LA was in the midst of a sustained, debilitating heat wave: parched from a years-long drought. The church to which I was headed for 5:30 pm Mass that day had no A/C.

I wheeled into the parking lot just a teeny tad late. Mostly I'm on time and I'm never ten minutes late, but I will more often than is perhaps strictly necessary be late by, say, a minute and a half. I'm not proud of it, but that's how I sometimes roll. This is due to a habit, perhaps a compulsion I have, of not allowing myself quite enough time to get places and/or squeezing in one too many minor errands, and then careening through the streets and deriving huge satisfaction from arriving at my destination with ten seconds to spare. It's a stupid ego-based tic, an adrenaline hit, and a practice that is obviously not terribly cognizant of others.

I hadn't run any errands before Mass that day, but I was coming straight from the gym. I still had on a workout top, blue. I also had on a pair of Diesel jeans, a nice belt, silver earrings and a bracelet, and Mephisto sandals. My nails were done. So I wasn't dressed like a street person (which is okay, obviously, if you are a street person). But I was rushed, and my hair, as is its, or my wont, was a bit disheveled, and my tank top, sleeveless, was perhaps a bit tighter than we all might wish. As I was dashing from my car into church, the thought did cross my mind that maybe I should put on the long-sleeved shirt I had in the trunk.

But as I said, I was late already and the temperature was over 100 and I figured I'd slip in, sit in the back, and all would be well.

So I crept in during the first reading and sat in the back. The sanctuary was sweltering and the ladies were all fanning themselves with rolled-up bulletins and missalettes. It was Tuesday, which meant Adoration afterwards, which I fully planned to stay for. That made me happy, and being at Mass, any Mass, always makes me happy, and I had always liked this particular church where for years I'd frequently attended the 5:30 p.m. daily Mass.

I'd been coming for years and my fellow parishioners tolerated me but no-one had ever gone out of their way to say hi. That was okay. As a single woman of a certain age, I'm used to smiling at people in church and not having them smile back. Plus Caucasians at this parish were a very distinct minority.

Right away I also noticed: a new priest! Mid-thirties to early forties. Earnest. Beautiful singing voice. Filipino perhaps, as was much of the parish. Said the liturgy slowly. Lovely all around.

I pondered all these things in my heart during the readings and homily. When it came time for the Eucharist. I made my way down the aisle, singing "Pan de Vida" with the others.

I was in the right-hand line, the side on which the new priest was standing. When I got up to the front, I held out the little throne I'd made of my hands to receive the Eucharist, as I always do.

The priest placed the Host in my hand.

He said, "The Body of Christ" as usual.

Then he leaned toward me with the most welcoming, beatific smile and said something else.

For a second, I simply couldn't compute. For those of you who may not be Catholic, the priest never *ever* speaks to you during Communion.

My God! I thought. *Does the man read my blog? Does he recognize me? Is he trying to tell me he likes my column in the archdiocesan newspaper?*

Here again, I'm not proud, but I just couldn't imagine any other possible explanation.

I stood there uncertainly for a second, smiling, and whispered, "What?"

And the priest leaned forward and very slowly, very clearly, said— "Please dress appropriately next time you come to Mass."

Does that not trump all? Is that not absolutely 100% beyond genius?

I was stunned, I was shocked, I made my way back to my pew, pulsating with embarrassment but also strangely…exultant.

I did have a split-second of wanting to turn back and say, "Dude, these jeans cost a hundred and twenty-five bucks."

I did have a half-second of wanting to say, "Here I have trudged to Mass, bravely, loyally, alone, for [at the time] close to twenty years." *Good for you*, my true self whispered: *So dress appropriately*.

Part of me wanted to protest, "I come to this church where after years no-one knows who I am, no-one cares, no-one knows I write for that *Magnificat* they're toting. Still, I feel connected to them. I pray for them. I'm grateful for them." That voice again: *Good for you: So dress appropriately for Mass*.

I often joked that I was the only white Catholic in hipster Silver Lake where I then lived: *Very funny, so show your respect for the people of color who sit beside you in the pews by dressing appropriately next time you come to Mass*.

I nipped those self-justifying thoughts in the bud, in other words, and I'll tell you why. Because, when push came to shove, all those years of prayer and of trudging to Mass and of schlepping to Confession had formed in me the habit of obedience. In spite of my many faults, my fidelity had formed in me a basically humble and contrite heart.

Thus the exultation. Ever since coming into the Church I'd been waiting for Christ to speak to me. And now, I realized, he had.

St. Francis of Assisi heard, "Rebuild my church." Mother Teresa heard, "Wouldst thou not help?" I heard, "Put on a decent shirt and comb your hair."

Seriously, at once I took the message as coming straight from Christ. That priest had seen straight through to my core, to my central conflict, to the way I was still trying to serve both God and mammon.

To wit: at the time, I'd been single for 15 years. That's hard sometimes. Usually I'm okay, but when I feel rejected or abandoned or anxious or afraid, I do tend to want a little more than usual to be seen. Something had happened the day before that had made me feel rejected. I had been craving, subconsciously at least, a little male attention.

That someone *had* seen me—Christ—wasn't lost on me for a second.

The priest's words touched as well on many other unfortunate tendencies of mine. To think the rules are made for everyone but me. To think," Oh but my heart *yearns*—why should I care what my hair looks like?" My impatience. My tendency to use what can border on frenetic activity to anesthetize emotional pain.

Later in the week I told the story, perhaps unwisely, to a lapsed Catholic friend. Right away, she rolled her eyes and asked, "Don't you think the priest might have been prompted by his own unworked-through stuff?" "No I don't," I said firmly. "I don't care what his hang-ups are and I don't care what his politics are. He was right. You show respect for Christ."

Later still I thought of the Parable of the Great Banquet (Matthew 22:1-14; Luke14:15-24) and realized: *I didn't have on my wedding garment that day*. By wedding garment I don't mean some weird kind of pre-Vatican II chapel veil which for me would be a terrible affectation and I couldn't wear for two seconds without obsessing, "Is everybody noticing how holy I am?"

No, the real wedding garment is largely inner. The real wedding garment is doing things nobody's going to notice. Leaving on time. Taking a few minutes of silence to prepare for Mass. Cultivating the humility and love constantly to be aware that our appearance, demeanor, and capacity to be present affect the people around us. That doesn't mean we have to look dowdy.

It means that, whatever our station in life, our heart is oriented toward motherhood, in the deepest sense of the word.

It meant that, in my Mephisto sandals, silver earrings and nice jeans, I got to be the bride of Christ.

I was always telling Jesus how much I loved him. It's as if he were saying now, as he said to Peter in John 21:15-17:

"Do you? Lovest me thou more than these?"

"Yes, Lord, you know that I love you."

"Feed my lambs."

"Lovest thou me?"

"Yes, Lord, you know that I love you."

"Feed my sheep."

"Heather, lovest thou me"

"Lord, you know everything; you know that I love you."

"Then feed my sheep."

And dress appropriately for Mass.

 THE ETERNAL CHILD

"[A]s it is expressed by the 'puer eternus' (eternal child) of the collective unconscious, there exists a connection between childhood and resurrection, and Hope brings the grace that we anticipate from Easter." *

—JEAN BASTAIRE, FROM THE PREFACE TO CHARLES PÉGUY'S *THE PORTAL OF THE MYSTERY OF HOPE*

One weekday afternoon several winters ago I drove down Cesar Chavez Ave. to LA's Chinatown for the purpose of getting a $20 foot massage.

The notion of a massage of any kind is foreign to my thrifty Yankee upbringing. My Calvinist impulse when in pain is to push harder, work more, soldier through. That's what my father, a bricklayer did; that's what my mother (to eight kids) did. Only lately had I allowed myself to realize that my entire body was killing me; even then, I'd had to gradually work up to the idea of "treating" myself to a (low-end) foot massage.

To compensate for this unseemly pampering I parked a half mile away, even though it was raining: partly so as to avoid paying a meter or, God forbid, a lot; partly because I like building a little penance into my pleasure.

I enjoyed walking in the drizzle through the deserted streets: the pastry shops, the dim sum palaces, the noodle joints, the workman squatting against a storefront with a Styrofoam container of roast duck and rice, the downtown skyscrapers looming in the mist…

"Foot massage" in LA is a term of art, an hour-long affair that includes a neck, back, shoulder and leg rub. The place was about what you'd expect for 20 bucks: dim lights, tiny rooms, sitar Muzak. First I got to soak my feet in a tub of nice warm water while "Lisa" did my neck and back. Then I reclined in a big, comfy towel-covered chair while she knelt and did my legs and then my feet.

Almost as soon as she started on my calves, I began crying. When you are never touched, to have someone touch you, someone who doesn't want anything and is coming from a basic place of warmth unleashes, for me anyway, a cascade of emotions. That you can walk through the anonymous streets of a city and through a particular door and someone will allow you, for a price, but still, to take off your shoes and socks and will then touch you, will not shame you, will not ask you to give an account of yourself, will not be—or at least not act—repulsed, is really, I have to say, a kind of poignant gift from what often seems an unfeeling world.

We carry in our bodies a whole range of wounds: of hurt, of loneliness, of the continual daily onslaught of tiny slights and insults, of guilt for the slights and insults we impose on others. If you're single, you carry the added weight, the secret shame, of knowing that that you are first in no-one's heart. You walk the earth with billions of other people and you are first in no human being's heart. As I age, I'm finding, what also comes up is a primal fear of appearing to be debilitated, weak, in need of help; a deep primordial limbic terror of being cast out of the herd and left to die, alone.

I'd somewhat come to terms with all that, though, and what I was really thinking of, as Lisa worked over my at the moment deteriorating-in-various ways feet, was my mother. Mom was in a home at the time in Dover, New Hampshire with Alzheimer's. She'd been in the same second-floor corner room for four years, quite proud that she could still navigate the stairs; insistently, even defiantly (that's my Mom!), refusing to use a walker. But she'd been failing, as we inevitably do.

Mom, the most fastidious person I know, had been having trouble cleaning herself. Mom, who put her whole life on hold to sit by the metaphorical telephone, to be on call in case someone needed her, could no longer hear the phone ringing, even though it was two feet away. "Well hello there," she'll say to my brother Geordie, who lives closest by and bears the brunt of visiting, accompanying to doctor's visits, and decision-making. "She knows I'm friend, not foe," he'll report, "but that's about it. She greets me about the way she would the plumber."

Mom took a little fall on the stairs recently, plus she's started getting belligerent (also wildly out of character: Mom's stubborn but she's also extremely non-confrontational), and the short of it is that last week the people at the home made her move in downstairs, next to the nurse's station, with a roommate.

I can't really describe how very much my mother 1) resists change and 2) is not a roommate person. We all thought she'd freak; instead, and this may be a measure of her diminishment: she didn't blink an eye. She expressed initial surprise—"Why didn't you tell me yesterday?"—and then went meekly, happily along. So far, so good, for which we are grateful.

Still—it's my mother. I'm her firstborn, and it's my mother. All week I'd been thinking of the Gospel passage, "Amen, amen, I say to you, when you were younger, you used to dress yourself and go where you wanted; but when you grow old, you will stretch out your hands, and someone else will dress you and lead you where you do not want to go" [John 21:18].

And here in this dim massage room, I thought as well of a story a friend had recently told me about when she'd been in rehab. She said her roommate had been a burn victim, a fellow alcoholic who'd tried to fry a hamburger one night when she was drunk and her dress had caught fire and she'd been too wasted to extinguish the flames or call 9-1-1 and had sustained third-degree burns over half her body.

This woman, the burn victim, would lie there with a pillow over her mouth in rehab and scream and scream and scream. The pillow somewhat muffled the sound but the terrible, haunting, wrenching anguish still came through. Finally my friend had said, "Is there something I can do? Are you all right?" And the burn-victim woman said, "Yeah, I'm okay. I'm screaming now because I was afraid if I screamed in the hospital, they wouldn't take care of me."

I was afraid if I screamed, they wouldn't take care of me. Isn't that on some level the wound we all carry? I thought of my mother, raised on a Rhode Island chicken farm during the Depression with a mother who literally went days without saying a word, and a father who up and left one day when my mother was 13, never to return, only to surface years later with a new, second family.

I thought how maybe she'd been afraid to scream all her life because, even as she'd remained silent, no-one had adequately cared for her. I thought how when your whole psyche has been formed by neglect and abandonment, you are maybe subconsciously afraid that your own child will reject you. I thought of how, in many ways, I had rejected her.

I thought about all the people I have been hurt by in my life who couldn't or wouldn't get closer, and how maybe in fact they had exercised a superhuman amount of courage and heart to allow themselves even to get as close as they had.

I thought of how, like my mother, I am so not a roommate person and yet, a year and a half ago, partly due to the Depression we were then going through, I'd gotten a roommate, too.

"She still reads a little," Geordie had said of Mom. "I don't know how much she absorbs, but she had *The Wind in the Willows* out the other day."

I thought of how, last year, I too, had re-read *The Wind in the Willows* ("Ratty, please! I want to row, now!), a book my mother had first read to me and that we both loved. I'd even gone so far as to read a biography of author Kenneth Grahame——whose mother had died when he was five, whose father was an alcoholic, who had made an unhappy marriage, and whose only child, a son nicknamed Mouse, had been emotionally troubled all his life and committed suicide at the age of twenty by throwing himself beneath a train.

I thought of how Geordie had told me, "Mom has two books by her bed, the Bible and *Parched*"——my first memoir.

Could any daughter, any writer, hope for a greater tribute? I thought "In the beginning was the Word," and of how, before I'd been able to find my way to an actual church, books were the closest thing to a church I had. I thought of how my mother had wanted to be a writer, and how in a way I became one for her.

I thought of all the time in my life I had spent thinking, *If only my mother had hugged me, if only my mother had told me I was pretty, if only my mother had* ...and how, on the cusp of late middle age, I had finally come to realize that of all the mothers in the world, I had gotten the perfect one, the only one, the best one.

The one who had taught me to love books and silence and trees. The one whose secret sorrows and wounds I had absorbed through my DNA. The one who I been afraid to scream in front of all my life because I was afraid she wouldn't take care of me.

But who *had* taken care of me, I saw now, had taken care of me and loved me and seen what was good in me and guided me toward what was important—integrity, kindness, humility—as no-one else could have.

I made no sound, though my face was wet with tears. I felt my mother—forever first in my heart, as our mothers always are—in my bones and blood and aching muscles. I felt her across the miles and the years. I felt her: the person who had known me longer than anyone on earth, though she no longer recognized me; who'd known me before I'd been born and would know me after we both died. I thought of how maybe the deepest cry of our hearts, no matter how old we are, if we are stripped right down to the bone, is "Mum! Mummy!"...

"Do you want some hot tea?" Lisa asked afterward but that would have been too much intimacy, too much indulgence maybe, so I said no, but thank you so much, and got dressed, and left.

It was raining harder now and I pulled my coat around me a little tighter and put on my scarf. Homeless people were sleeping along Cesar Chavez, huddled in damp sleeping bags, their belongings getting soaked.

I'd planned on heading straight back to my car. But on an impulse, I found myself walking first west, and then south over the 101 freeway to the Cathedral of Our Lady of the Angels.

I would go inside and sit for a while. I would kneel and pray.

Puddles pooled in the courtyard. I paused before the tall

entrance doors and raised my eyes to the Mary, sculpted in bronze, who stood silently, palms open to the world, above.

Guardian of the poor.

Mother of all lost children.

Like us, perpetually awaiting Easter.

ENDNOTES

II. POOR BABY

As the Swiss mystic and philosopher Father Maurice Zundel observed:

"We are not interchangeable"...

Maurice Zundel, *With God In Our Daily Life*, (Québec City: Éditions Pauline, 1993), 77-78.

III. THE HOLY FAMILY

PRAISE THE MUTILATED WORLD

And perhaps the sexes are more related than we think, and the great renewal of the world will perhaps consist in this...

Rainer Maria Rilke, *Letters to a Young Poet*, trans. M.D. Herter Norton (New York: W.W. Norton & Company, 1934), 29-30.

WHEN IN ROME, WALK THE TIBER

An incident from the life of Dorothy expresses well what I am trying to say here. Dorothy went to Rome during the Second Vatican Council...

Catherine Doherty, *Poustinia: Encountering God in Silence, Solitude and Prayer* (Combermere, ON: Madonna House Publications, 2000), 27-28.

The Son of Man did not solve all the sad problems of sex. For those who wish to follow him...

François Mauriac , *Life of Jesus* (Chicago: The Thomas More Press, 1936 (1978 edition)), 156-157.

THE PARADISE OF SEXUAL REVOLUTION

Visit a prison and ask the men in the cell blocks to recount their sexual histories, and those of their mothers and fathers...

Anthony Esolen, from the essay "The Paradise of Sexual Revolution," published February 17, 2012 by The Witherspoon Institute's "Public Discourse": http://www.thepublicdiscourse.com/2012/02/4756/.

OUR CATACLYSMIC, LIFE-GIVING YES

But as the writer Madeleine L'Engle once observed, "We do not draw people to Christ by loudly discrediting what they believe"...

Madeleine L'Engle, *Walking on Water: Reflections on Faith and Art* (Colorado Springs: WaterBrook, 2001), 140-141

Contemplative monk Erasmo Leiva-Merikakis (now known as Brother Simeon) wrote: "Léon Bloy...once said"...

Erasmo Leiva-Merikakis, *Love's Sacred Order: The Four Loves Revisited* (San Francisco: Ignatius Press, 2000), 163.

As writer Alice McDermott notes, "Being a Catholic is an act of rebellion"...

Alice McDermott, from the essay "The Lunatic in the Pew: Confessions of a Natural-Born Catholic," Boston College Magazine, Summer, 2003. http://bcm.bc.edu/issues/summer_2003/ft_natural.html.

IV. RADICAL FREEDOM, RADICAL EXILE

SECTION EPIGRAPH

In order to be free you simply have to be so, without asking permission of anybody... You have to have your own hypothesis about what you are called to do, and follow it...

Andrei Tarkovsky, *Sculpting in Time* (New York: Harper & Row, 1973), 100.

SAINTHOOD: TO WILL THE ONE THING

I was running someone down [to a priest], saying beastly things of him. Suddenly I noticed that [the priest's] eyes were shut...

Maisie Ward, *That Divine Eccentric* (London: Sheed & Ward, 1962), 151.

In a review of the book *Caryll Houselander and the Flowering of Christ*, Dr. Janet Golden observes: "[Houselander] is that rarity among Catholic writers"...

Janet Golden, "Caryll Houselander and the Flowering of Christ": http://
www.catholicculture.org/culture/library/view.cfm?id=188, originally

published in October, 1954 by The Missionary Society of St. Paul the
Apostle, in a larger work entitled *Catholic World*.

THE SPIRITUALITY OF IMPERFECTION

Originally, in conformity with the family pattern, she had felt
that if she did displease her father…

Joseph F. Schmidt, FSC, *Everything is Grace: The Life and Way of Thérèse of Lisieux*
(Ijamsville, MD: The Word Among Us Press, 2007), 125.

Thérèse was pleasing her father, but not because she needed to
please him
in order to make herself feel connected and good…

Joseph F. Schmidt, FSC, *Everything is Grace: The Life and Way of Thérèse of Lisieux*
(Ijamsville, MD: The Word Among Us Press, 2007), 127.

[I]f their sublime dignity raises them above the angels," as she
diplomatically put it, "they are nonetheless weak and fragile
men."

St. Thérèse of Lisieux, Robert J. Edmonson, trans., *The Story of a Soul: A New
Translation* (Brewster, MA: Paraclete Press, 2006), 134."

THE BANQUET TABLE

There is great satisfaction in remaining faithful; perhaps it is the greatest satisfaction of all. Even if not one knows about your faithfulness, even if no one values it.

Aleksandr Solzhenitsyn, *Cancer Ward*, trans. Nicholas Bethell and Nicholas Burg (New York: FSG Classics, 2015), 350.

THE GOOD FATHERS

People say that there is a scarcity of priests. In truth, what an adorable mystery it is that there still are priests...

François Mauriac, *Holy Thursday: An Intimate Remembrance*, from "Holy Orders," Chapter Five (Manchester, NH: Sophia Institute Press, 1991).

It is easy for any child to pick out the faults of the sermon on his way home from Church every Sunday...

Flannery O'Connor, *The Habit of Being: Letters of Flannery O'Connor* (New York: Farrar, Straus & Giroux, 1979), 307-308.

THE ETERNAL CHILD

[A]s it is expressed by the 'puer eternus' (eternal child) of the collective unconscious...

Jean Bastaire, from the preface to Charles Péguy's *The Portal of the Mystery of Hope* (Grand Rapids, MI: Wm. B. Eerdmans Publishing Co., 2005), xiv.

ACKNOWLEDGMENTS

Special thanks to Timothy P. Flanigan, infectious disease doctor extraordinaire, brother in Christ, and fellow lover of adventure and fun. His generosity helped make the publication of *RAVISHED* possible.

Parts of the manuscript were written at the Dorland Mountain Arts Colony in Temecula, California. Thanks to the good people there as well, who through the years have provided sanctuary, sunsets, and stellar pebble-collecting.

Made in United States
Orlando, FL
05 February 2022

14496662R00114